D0847818

39969000390840

Kentucky Bred

Kentucky Bred

A CELEBRATION OF THOROUGHBRED BREEDING

BY DAN WHITE

Photography by Jon Naso

 A MOUNTAIN LION BOOK

Taylor Publishing Company
Dallas, Texas

Copyright © 1986 by Mountain Lion, Inc.

All rights reserved.
No part of this publication may be reproduced
in any form, or by any means, without permission
in writing from the publisher.

Library of Congress Cataloging-in-Publication Data

White, Dan, 1943–
   Kentucky bred.

   1. Thoroughbred horse.   2. Race horses—Kentucky.
3. Horse-racing—Kentucky.   I. Title.
SF293.T5W47 1986   798.4   86-1947
ISBN 0-87833-529-3

Printed in the United States of America
9 8 7 6 5 4 3 2 1

BOOK DESIGN BY LURELLE CHEVERIE

To Lisa and David

Contents

"Let's brush 'em out, get 'em looking nice for the company."

"Good morning, folks. Take a look and just let my boys know which horses you'd like to see."

"He's a nice foal, a first foal. He was big and awkward but he's started to come into himself. He's come so quickly, who knows where he might go."

"She looks like an athlete, a runner, not a weight lifter."

"I don't like the knee."

"That horse has the longest legs, looks like a goddamned giraffe."

"The perfect-looking ones don't run."

"That one walks as if he had flippers on."

Getting Ready for Company

"Last year, that colt went for $700,000. That ain't potato chips."
"This ain't no dairy sale."

"Horse coming through—excuse me, folks."
"Ooooh, he's beautiful. Look how shiny his coat is."
"Don't walk behind that horse, please."
"He looks just like his ol' man."
"Keep your eye on Hip #215—he's a son of Nijinsky II and could fetch a big price."
"Please, move aside so we can get this horse through."

Hip #215, a bay colt who is half brother to Kentucky Derby winner Seattle Slew (1977), has been led onto the plaza outside the sales pavilion at Keeneland Stables in Lexington, Kentucky. The second day of Keeneland's annual summer sale of selected yearlings is in progress. It is the premier event of its kind in the world. In a few minutes, the colt will be taken inside to the auction ring. It is expected he will bring the highest price of the auction, certain to be a multimillion-dollar bid. The crowd gathers around to admire the colt. For a short while longer, his name will remain Hip #215, the number on the small sticker on his rump.

He is one of more than 420 well-bred, meticulously groomed Thoroughbreds that await their turn in the auction ring during this preeminent sale. These blue-bloods include sons and daughters of Seattle Slew and Northern Dancer, two of the world's most coveted sires, and brothers, sisters, half brothers and half sisters to countless millionaires and champions. Twelve yearlings by Northern Dancer sold for an average price of $3.44 million last year at Keeneland. One of his sons—Snaafu Dancer out of My Bupers—commanded a world-record $10.2 million during the 1983 summer sale. Yearlings by Seattle Slew, the leading sire of 1984, have proven very popular in the sales ring, too. Last year, one of his daughters, Alchaasibiyeh out of Fine Prospect, sold for $3.75 million, a world record for a filly. Altogether, buyers paid $175,932,000 for 313 yearlings at the 1984 Keeneland sale, an average of $544,681.

Horses purchased during previous Keeneland sales have been extremely successful on the track, both at home and abroad. Tank's Prospect, which sold during the 1983 sale, won the Preakness this past year. Shadeed, Al Bahathri, and Triptych, three more graduates

of the '83 sale, won classic races in Europe. The quality of the horses, the reputation of the sale, and the spectacle itself— all are part of the mystique of the Kentucky-bred Thoroughbred. That mystique has attracted to the sale buyers and agents, as well as the admiring and curious, from twenty-seven different countries, including the Far East and Australia. It is they who are referred to as the "company" by the stable hands and the yearling managers who have charge of the sale horses for the different farms.

Throughout the sale, and for the several days preceding the sale, and, in some cases, for as long as a week and more before, they have been touring the farms and stables around Lexington. They have been inspecting the horses, feeling their legs, and staring into their eyes, trying to divine whether the youngsters have the ability to win races, and ultimately to propagate more successful racehorses.

The American Stud Book, the registry maintained by The Jockey Club for all Thoroughbreds foaled in the United States and Canada, defines a yearling as a colt, filly, or gelding in its second calendar year of life (beginning January 1 of the year following its birth).

(A gelding is a male horse of any age that is unsexed—had both testicles removed.) Last year, more than 42,000 yearlings were foaled and registered as Thoroughbreds in this country and Canada. Of that number, fewer than 400 will win stakes races during their careers, about 1 percent of the total number. Of that equine elite, 27 percent will have been foaled in Kentucky, twice as many as any other state.

Hip #215's coat has been brushed to a rich glow. Its mane has been pulled over to one side. The hairs are as straight as teeth on a comb. Its tail has been fluffed, its hooves picked clean and polished dark. Six stable hands attend it. They each have soft cloths trailing from their back pockets. Just before the horse enters the sales ring, they will give it one last buffing.

The colt stands at ease, nuzzling the chest of the groom holding the lead chain, occasionally mouthing his hand. If he were an older, more mature stallion, or if he were more anxious about all the hoopla that has been taking place, he might bite the hand as a way of expressing his impatience with this endless standing about, but he is a playful youngster, and inclined to be in good spirits about all the attention he is getting. The groom jingles the chain continuously, exerting slight pressure on the bit, and reminding him with the noise that he, the groom, is in charge. The colt's shoulders and hind quarters are tapered and muscular. When the colt walks, ripples and bulges flow back and forth from head to tail. The symmetry of its motion is wondrous in its grace and power, and fearful in the strength of its hind legs, the thrust of its head and shoulders. The colt's ears are alert, cocked at an angle of 45 degrees with the body. That is an angle considered perfect by designers of perfect horses. Alert ears are thought to be a sign of intelligence, attentiveness; unmoving, limp ears, an indication of dullness; overly active ears, a possible sign of excitability and skittishness.

Its eyes are dark, likewise alert, not quite comprehending, but showing no fear. Many judges of horseflesh say the eyes are the windows to the soul of the animal. It is in the eyes that they can see the spirit of the horse, the size of its heart, the measure of its courage to run all-out.

And what do the dark eyes see? A procession of hats: panamas, golf caps, baseball caps, straw hats with wide brims, visors, bandannas worn by men and women alike who constitute the "company." Company has traveled to Keeneland by pickup truck,

by Mercedes, by private jet. Company includes ladies with parasols to filter the bright Kentucky sun, and women in suits and slacks and sun dresses, as immaculately coiffed as the horses. There are men in silk shirts and straw hats, jeans and boots, three-piece suits, tweed coats, and T-shirts.

And Arabs, with their bottomless pockets. Whole families from Australia, buyers over from England, from Ireland, from Hong Kong and Japan, back, greeting each other, old friends and acquaintances who haven't seen each other since the last yearling sale. Or since the Epsom Derby, or the Irish Sweeps Derby, or the Ladbrokes European Free Handicap, or Santa Anita.

Among them are the farm managers and the agents and the bankers and the lawyers, and the insurance men dispensing their cards as fast as they can get them out of their pockets. And the stable hands, liveried in matching outfits that represent the colors of the farms they work for. And there are the ''other'' stars, besides the horses: the television stars, the public dignitaries, the retired great athletes, the legendary old horse trainers, the current, most popular trainers. The stable hands try to pick out the celebrities. At day's end, they compare notes.

The procession of hats, sales catalogues in hand, pens dangling by chains from their necks, moves from barn to barn. They ask to see particular horses, to study their conformation. Each time they look at a horse, they pencil notes in their catalogues. Each yearling has a page of the catalogue that lists his pedigree and information about him.

The pedigrees of the men and women who study the horses are not as easily accessible. For the most part, the buyers at Keeneland represent immense fortunes. Old money and new money scrutinize the horses together. They are people who own trust funds and land and glass factories and corrugated-box factories and oil wells and shipping lines. They are used to having things their way. Yet, they cannot command a yearling to grow into a Kentucky Derby

champion. They expect results when they spend money but they can find no one who will guarantee results when they breed a Nijinsky colt to the mother of Seattle Slew. They are people in control who are fascinated by what they cannot control, what they cannot ordain, what they cannot predict, what they cannot prepare for. Except— to prepare as carefully as possible, to reduce the chance of failure. They know that with racehorses, they must defer ultimately to Nature and whatever alignment of planets and stars controls the destiny of these sleek half tons of muscle and sinew as they thunder down the racetrack. These often-beautiful, stylish people who control so much are fascinated by the gamble, by the mystique of gambling in a rarefied atmosphere where a broken leg or a stillborn foal can wipe out a million-dollar investment. And because money is not a problem to them, they go for the best. The best in the world of Thoroughbred horses is in Kentucky.

The barns are laid out in rows, an immense complex of army-style barracks. They are unlike any buildings an army post has ever seen. They are bright, cheerful, clean, of white cinder block, their tin roofs painted green. Many of the farms have decorated their assigned stalls by hanging pots of brightly colored mums and banners with the farm's name. Towering Chinese elms canopy the lawns between the barns. Each lawn has an oval walking path where the exercise boys show the horses to company. In the center of the lawns, candy-striped awnings shade benches where those who are flaked out can sit and watch the horses and watch the people who watch the horses. Swallows twitter back and forth to their hidden niches in the lofts of the barns. Horses whinny and snort. They are always notice-able—in sight and sound—no matter how thick the crowd, or how loud the clamor. Tubs of Coca-Cola have been placed at each pavilion. Black-tie waiters who have been hired by the farms mingle in the crowd throughout the day. If it is early enough in the morning, they carry trays of coffee and juice and pastries. If it is not too early, they serve bloody marys and cool sherbety lime drinks that spill over the sides of their glasses. The whole scene is cool and sherbety, at the same time bright and pastoral, a part of Kentucky life that could hardly seem more perfect.

All the farms and the horses are kept busy from dawn to dusk. By the end of the day, company will be tired. The exercise boys and stable hands will be bushed. The horses will be beat, fed up with

walking back and forth for company. Tired is a good feeling, however, because the mere presence of a yearling in this select sale means it will likely be sold at a considerable price.

Owners around the country and world nominate their yearlings, at $1,000 a clip, by March 1 of each year. Keeneland's pedigree committee considers each nominee. Only the best pedigrees are accepted. Keeneland then sends a team of veterinarians on the road to inspect the conformation of each entry. Many well-bred horses don't pass the conformation test. Keeneland has built its reputation on ''quality products.''

The yearling sales weren't always at Keeneland. Before 1943, Saratoga Springs in New York used to be the site of the principal yearling sales in this country. The sales were held during the annual race meetings there. But, in 1943, wartime travel restrictions made it impossible for Kentucky breeders to ship their horses north. At the same time, and for the same reason, the Saratoga race meeting was moved downstate to make it more accessible for racegoers from New York City. Keeneland, which had also closed down as a racetrack, offered its barns to the Kentucky breeders who normally would have sent their horses north to New York. The first sale in 1944 grossed $2,288,000, an average of $5,231 for each of the 437 colts and fillies in the sale. That figure would scarcely be enough for an opening bid in today's auction. Still, it was good money then for the consignors and the agents and it's big money now. Last year, one farm sold fourteen yearlings for $17,700,000, the largest sum received by a single consignor in the history of the sales. Two other farms sold eleven and thirteen yearlings for more than $12 million and $11 million, respectively.

The farms depend on the yearling sales for their profit for the year, and they compete for the buyers. Many sponsor lavish sales parties the weekend before the sales begin. They are parties that people talk about the rest of the year. They are parties where black-tie attendants greet guests at the turnoff from a highway and direct them along tree-shaded lanes that wind in and around vast fields of bluegrass pasture on which Thoroughbreds graze, their tails twitching. They don't seem to care about the arrival of so much company. The roads are bordered by white plank fences or limestone walls. Their journey is illumined by torches that line the road. Eventually, the compound of buildings and tents specially erected for the evening's festivities

appear. More attendants in black tie greet the guests, take their cars and park them, filling field after field. Under the tents, a feast has been spread out over beds of ice: lobster tails in their shells, jumbo shrimp, a cornucopia of vegetables, and then the roasts and the desserts and the wines and champagnes. A celebrity singer has been flown in to entertain until the early hours of the morning. He sings to everybody who is anybody in Lexington and in the horse world, which covers the whole world. It is very late before the company begins to think about the business of buying horses the next day.

Big money. For the citizens of Lexington and ultimately for the Commonwealth of Kentucky. The Thoroughbred industry in Kentucky will tell you it carries its own weight: It is a major source of taxes, jobs, and tourism. At least 20,000 jobs. More than $11 million just from racing revenues in 1984. The Thoroughbred industry accounts for millions of dollars invested each year in permanent land improvements that enhance the landscape and natural beauty of the state. It provides the incentive for hundreds of thousands of visitors, tourists, racing fans, and horse buyers to come to Kentucky each year.

The Commonwealth of Kentucky taxes the horse industry coming and going, thirteen different ways: a 5 percent sales tax on all horses sold at auction, except for breeding stock or horses less than two years old that are bought by nonresidents and shipped out of state. Every Kentucky resident who buys a Thoroughbred at public auction pays the required sales tax.

A 5 percent tax on stud fees.

A 5 percent tax on the price of all horses claimed at a Kentucky race meeting.

A tax on all horses, except breeding stock, bought out of state and returned to Kentucky.

A tax on feed.

On bedding.

On tack and supplies.

There are personal and corporate taxes; local property taxes; a tax on track licenses; occupational taxes; parimutuel taxes; and a tax on the cost of admission to the racetrack.

Altogether, tens of millions of dollars in taxes accrue to the benefit of the citizens of Kentucky as a result of the Thoroughbred industry.

And there are the jobs: Owner, trainer, and jockey obviously come

to mind first. There is also the breeder, the farm hand, the stable worker, the veterinarian, the blacksmith. There are feed and bedding suppliers, tack suppliers and vanning companies whose representatives sit poised behind a desk in the Keeneland sales pavilion ready to sell their services to the horses' new owners. There are the repairers of fences and barns, the bankers who specialize in equine finance, the lawyers who specialize in equine law, the brokers and agents, the realtors, the concessionaires, the advertisers, the printers, the hotels and restaurants, and the black-tie attendants. In the rarefied world of big-time financing, horses are capital assets, commodities, and tax shelters. They are affected by the price of oil in Dubai or Kuwait. In the more mundane world of tourists and shopkeepers and small manufacturers, horses become pewter and brass and ceramic figures, rocking chairs, cigarette lighters, bottle openers, lamps, door knockers, weather vanes, pins, badges, buttons, key fobs, placemats, fire pokers, and bookends. They adorn playing cards, dinner plates, light switches, glasses, stationery, and posters. A tourist in Kentucky can wipe his face with a towel bearing the image of a Thoroughbred, wrap his neck with a scarf of a Derby winner, drink from a mug with a picture of a horse, wrap a present for a friend at home in paper printed with galloping horses, and, for that one particular friend, purchase a toilet seat with the giant head of a Thoroughbred staring up. It's a billion-dollar industry. At the center of it are the top stallions and broodmares in the world quartered among some 1,200 farms. Most of those farms lie within a twenty-mile radius of the plaza that Hip #215 is standing on outside the sales pavilion at Keeneland.

With the stakes so high, preparation for the sale begins very early, early in the life of the horse, early in the spring before the summer sale, and early each day of the sale. Beginning in March or April, the yearlings will get corn oil and flax seed mixed in with their feed to give their coats a shine. They're kept out of the sun in their stalls during the day and only let out in the paddocks at night. Otherwise, the sun will bleach out the color in their coats. No horse that ever starred on television or in the movies knew different treatment. By the time of Kentucky Derby Week in May, it's really important to get hold of the yearlings that are to be sold and primp them up. Trainers start them on exercise routines, hand walking them for 30–45 minutes a day, getting them used to the chifney, a brass ring bit. They step up the grooming. During the last week, they pull their manes, clip the hairs off their faces, and have them reshoed. They want the horses to look sleek and muscular, not plump, not underfed, not tired. The yearlings have learned to "stand" by the time they arrive at Keeneland, legs slightly astraddle to show off their musculature, their conformation.

The yearlings are vanned to Keeneland several days before the sale to get settled into their temporary stalls, and to be available to be seen by buyers.

Preparation for the coming of company begins when the nightwatchman in the stables completes his last round of the stalls and notices the first streak of gray in the dark sky. Simultaneously, the stable hands begin arriving in their cars and trucks, mumbling muted greetings, jacketed against a slight chill, still mostly asleep. There is a saying that people who show up at 7:00 a.m. to tend to their horses don't have good horses. Everyone at Keeneland figures he has good horses, for the entire compound is awake and moving by 5:00. The walkers take the horses out into the dark and lead them around and around the paths in a labor-intensive routine that technology has yet to change. The yearlings, penned up all night in their stalls, are stiff and cramped, eager to be walking. Each groom walks silently, catching his last ten winks of sleep. They shake the lead chain when they feel the horse's head strain in the wrong direction. They speak to soothe the animal, or to chastize it. They regard the yearlings as children who must be both loved and scolded: "Come on, little cupcake. . . ." and "Goddam it, do that again and I'll smack you. . . ."

The crews mucking out the stalls have stirred up the odor of urine and manure. Ammonia bites the nostrils. The aroma of hot coffee tries to soothe. Swallows scold the mucking crews as they rake out the old hay and pile it in big plastic tubs for removal. Fresh bales of hay and straw are stored above the stalls. The men flip them down and spread them out. Since the yearlings walk so much to show off for company, their morning exercise is short. They get just enough to stretch out and give the crews time to clean the stalls.

As soon as their walk is over, the horses receive the first of many groomings of the day. If a horse has collected a lot of dust the day before, he may get an early-morning washing. The stable hands bathe him from nose to stern with warm water and a mild detergent.

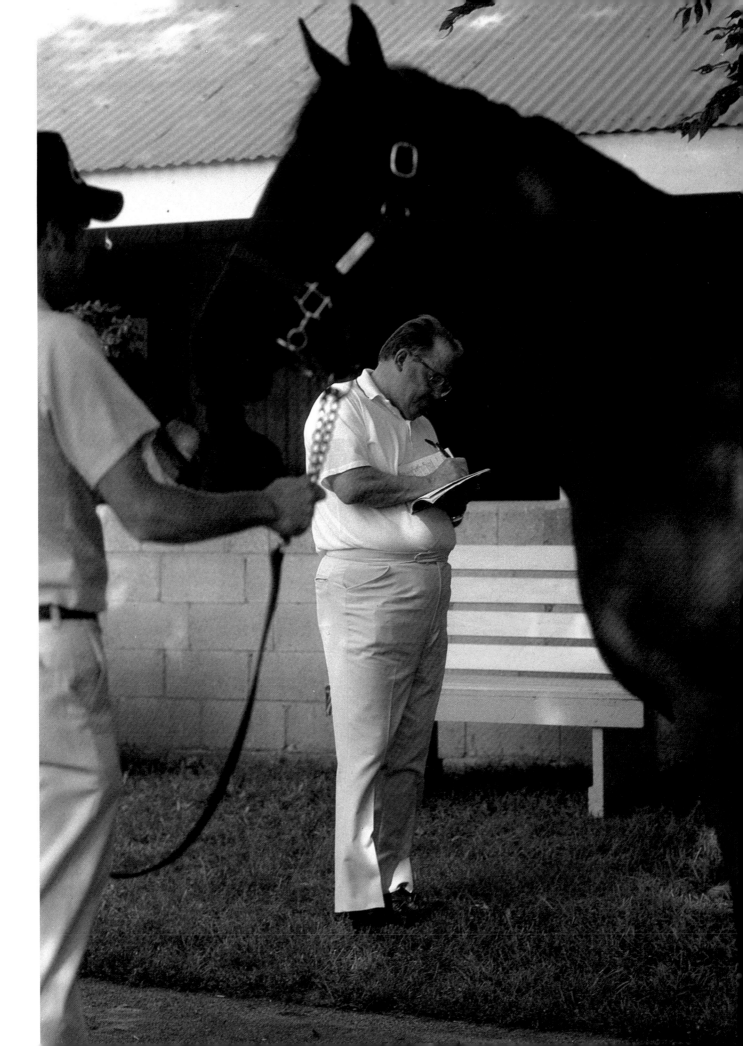

They move expertly over the great hidebound surfaces. Clouds
of vapor rise off the horse's back and are illuminated in the first light
of dawn. They brush from hard to soft, first lifting off the loose hair
and dust. They work down to the fluffy brushes which lay the hair
down and bring up a sheen that is noticeable, even in the meager
light. They pick the straw out of the tail, piece by piece. They gather
the tail by the handfuls, as if they were women separating their own
hair. They comb and brush it out until it is straight and fluffed.
It is a tail unlike anything the yearling's ancient, wild ancestor before
the time of man would have known. Shiny coats and fluffed tails are
among the benefits of having man around. There are others, but in
the grooming department, horses would generally be a mess of burrs
and skin abrasions and dirty, festering sores. The horse evolved with
more interest in using its tongue to assist in grazing and masticating
its food than in cleaning its anatomy.

Gentle is the groom who sponges the horse's eyes and nostrils,
cleaning out the duck butter, as some call it. Some of the yearlings
resist like little children. They scrunch their faces. They pull their

heads and snort, or lift their legs as if to kick. If they do that, they get
a quick slap on the rear from the groom, or a jerk on the bit. Each
hoof is inspected for grit and pebbles and caked dirt, which could
lead to irritation and soreness and lameness, not what company
wants to buy. Last thing the groom does is wipe the horse with
Absorbine Showsheen, a hair polish, and cover the hooves with a
dressing made up of pine tar and fish oil to keep the hooves soft and
flexible for growth.

Back in their stalls, the yearlings eat breakfast, one of three meals
they get each day. The grooms and stable hands head for the track
kitchen and some heavy work on biscuits and eggs and sausage and
waffles that will have to hold them until late that night. By 7:30 a.m.
the hoofprints in the cinder paths have been raked out, and the barn
areas spruced up. The old straw and hay have disappeared. It's time
to kill time until company comes. Time for everyone to catch up on
yesterday's racing news from the *Daily Racing Form,* which
materializes out of thin air and is as much a feature of the horse world
as straw and manure. The owner arrives to confer with his sales
manager and huddles off in the corner. In an hour or so, company
will begin to show.

There are two bad things that can happen to company at
Keeneland, and both can happen at the same time. One is that
company can spend a lot of money on a horse that turns out to be a
pelter, a snide, a plug, a worthless horse. The other is that company
can get kicked in the head by any one of several different horses
being led by nervous grooms through the huge throng that crowds
the paddocks throughout the sale. From time to time, an anxious colt
will rear up on its hind legs, and the crowd will scatter for safety from
the hooves. The crowd learns quickly that when a horse swings its
rear, it is not asking to be patted but positioning itself to kick.

Watching for equine traffic and staying clear of hind legs is the
easier task. Short of ensuring that the yearlings are of high pedigree
and meet basic standards of good conformation, little can be done to
guard against the risk of spending money on a good-looking horse
and discovering later that it's another nag. Still, they try. As the stable
hands walk the horses up and down the paths, the buyers stand and
watch them from all different angles—from the rear, the front, the side.
Is the line from the top of his leg to the center of his hoof nice and

MARSHALL COUNTY PUBLIC LIBRARY
1003 POPLAR STREET
BENTON, KENTUCKY 42025

straight, or do his legs stick out into another county? They look for looseness in the shoulders, for balance in the overall proportions of a horse. They watch the hips move, whether they swing loosely, easily. Are the legs going to hit when he runs? Is his hind end too wide? Do his feet pronate, or is he pigeon-toed? Is he sickle-hocked? Where do his feet land when he walks? A Thoroughbred's legs are made of glass. Buyers run their hands down the backs of the front legs, feeling for swollen tendons, or tiny chips, or funny knobs. They are among the tiny imperfections that could ruin a million-dollar investment. A yearling's knees are not yet closed. The buyer checks the size of the openings. He picks up each hoof and looks for irregular wear that might indicate unnatural stress on the feet. They check the mouth. A horse with a parrot's mouth, an overbite, could have difficulty chewing food, trouble digesting. And they look at the eyes and ears and any one of a dozen other secret telltale signs that might reveal spirit and character. And all the while, they scribble notes in their sales catalogues and talk in hushed undertones, off away from the crowd. The ethics of horse viewing are that no one ever publicly badmouths a horse. A horse might be missing a leg, but it would be considered against the rules of conduct for anyone publicly to note such a defect. Sly, catty agents and trainers and others wanting to lessen enthusiasm for a particular horse have been known to study a horse carefully, then walk away shaking their heads, but they have not spoken aloud.

These and other questions form the test for conformation. And if the horse has perfect conformation and perfect pedigree, there is still no telling how it will perform until it gets into the starting gate, or until it has been in the starting gate several times. The legends and lore of horse racing abound with stories like that of John Henry. John Henry was foaled near Paris, Kentucky, just northwest of Lexington, in 1975. He was an ordinary-looking sort, sired by an obscure stallion named Ole Bob Bowers, who once sold for $900. His dam, Once Double, had never produced much, either. From the start, no geometry known to man could have produced a straight line from his shoulders to his hooves—he stood well back at the knees and veterinarians classified him as a high risk, too liable to break down under the stress of racing. His future in doubt, he sold at the Keeneland winter sale for $1,100. To complicate matters, he was rank, or excessively sexual as a young stallion, which made him hard to train, so he was castrated. He was sold again, then again, before he finally began a racing career that would make him the all-time leading money winner, earning more than $6.5 million. He won thirty-nine of eighty-three races including his last four starts. He was second fifteen times, third nine times, and was one of only two Thoroughbreds ever to win a major stakes at the age of nine. He never seemed affected by his back-at-the-knees stance.

There are others:

– Count Fleet (Kentucky Derby winner in 1943) was pigeon-toed.

– Northern Dancer (Derby winner in 1964) was considered a runt, measuring at the withers a little over fifteen hands, compared to the average size for a Thoroughbred stallion of sixteen hands (a hand is approximately four inches).

Veteran trainers and owners will tell you the perfect ones don't run. And, they might add, the most expensive ones don't necessarily win:

– In 1976, one of the first yearlings ever to sell at $1 million was from Secretariat's first crop of yearlings. Named Canadian Bound, he placed second once in four starts and was retired to stud, where he has earned $4,770 in stud fees on the low price of $1,000, live foal guarantee.

– In 1979, Hoist the Kind, a yearling, sold for $1.6 million; unraced as a two- and three-year-old, unplaced in six starts as a four-year-old; sent to stud in Japan.

– Sailor King, by Nijinsky II, for $1.4 million in 1979; unraced at two and three, now at stud in Florida.

– A filly by Seattle Slew named Sumaya, one second place finish at three years, not raced as a four-year-old.

– Foxboro, $4.25 million son of Northern Dancer, unraced at two, unplaced as a three-year-old.

– And the world's most expensive yearling, Snaafi Dancer, $10.2 million at Keeneland in 1983, still has not raced.

The dice roll the other way. There are enough relatively rags-to-riches stories to round out the history of horse appraising.

– Spectacular Bid, Kentucky Derby winner in 1979, bought at Keeneland's September yearling sale for $37,000; earned $2.7 million.

– Seattle Slew, bought at sale for $17,500 in 1975. Won the Triple Crown in 1977 and now has an insurable worth of $140 million.

– Spend a Buck, bought privately for $12,500. Won the Kentucky
Derby in 1985 and has earned, to date, more than $3.3 million.

It is these latter stories that fan the hopes of those who are not big
enough frogs for the pond at Keeneland. By the same token, the
stories of disappointment and despair—well, the owner who can't

afford financially and emotionally to walk away from disaster and start over again is in the wrong game. Most know the stakes, and those who don't, find out quickly.

In the sales pavilion, a battalion of custodians leans into their mops. Others clean the windows that separate the theaterlike auditorium from the lobby and concourse areas. Still others wipe the curved rows of chairs that have been reserved for the buyers. Their names have been printed on slips of paper and inserted into the backs of the chairs. They represent a United Nations assembly of who's who in the international world of horsemen: Buckland Farm, Bluegrass Heights, Glen Hill Farm, Miller Farm, Kinderhill Farm, Prince Faisal, Prince Yazid, Spendthrift Farm, Three Chimneys Farm, Stavros Niarchos, Bright View Farm, Robert Sangster, BBA Ireland, BBA England, Lion Crest Stable, Cromwell Bloodstock, Leslie Combs, London Thoroughbred, Tom Gentry Farm, Dan Issel, Dave Parrish,

Brushwood Stables, Dogwood Stable, D.W. Lukas, Gainsborough Farm, Eugene Klein, Seth Hancock—Claiborne Farm, Narvile Inter, King Ranch, A.J. Foyt Jr., Luigi Mighietti, Mint Tree Stable, Amerinvest Thoroughbreds, Wimbledon Farms, Mrs. A.C. Dupont Jr., Rene Romanet, Warner L. Jones, Preston Madden, E. Colombo, Loblolly Stable, Laz Barrera, Mort Fink, Buck Pond Farm, Fabio Nove . . . .

In the lunchrooms off the concourse, countermen slice and pile stacks of corned beef and roast beef. Walkie-talkie radios crackle with questions and instructions from other parts of the compound. Someone is needed to begin sweeping the walks outside. Someone else to water down the mulch in the auction ring, where the horses stand while they are being bid on. Quickly, smoothly, the whole enterprise repairs itself from the day's preceding sale and prepares to move forward at the appointed hour of 1 p.m., when the sales auction will begin again.

Money has already begun changing hands at Keeneland. The attendant on duty in the parking lot adjacent to the sales pavilion and the barns presides over a domain that many want to occupy, but few are chosen. Only veterinarians and blacksmiths and owners and a few others are allowed into his tiny principality. He has secured it with sawhorses set across each parking space. When he moves a sawhorse so that a car can park, it is yet another example of an economic benefit provided by the Thoroughbred horse industry to the citizens of Kentucky, if not to the Commonwealth. As each grateful new member of this exclusive lot leaves his car, he palms a bill or two into the hands of the attendant. When the stakes are millions of dollars, a couple of bucks for a special parking space is part of the mystique. More so than the cars. A well-to-do horse buyer or owner cannot be identified by his car. The machines owned by the stable hands are far more indicative of the industry. They range from fancy doodad pickup trucks to rusty old buckets papered over with bumper stickers about horses like: "Have you hugged your horse today?" "I like Kentucky bred."

At five minutes to one, the auctioneer climbs to the podium in the sales pavilion and announces the bidding will begin at 1:00 sharp. The pavilion crowd is dense at the periphery, where the lunchrooms and lounges dispense the drinks and sandwiches. There is a happy buzz to the crowd. In the lounge, a section is reserved for buyers only. It is a haven whose ostensible purpose is to provide peace for

would-be buyers from the close scrutiny of the curious and the well-wishers and opposing bidders who search constantly for some hint of the next move.

At 1:00 sharp, the auctioneer starts right in, his bourbon-sweet voice intoning the mumbo jumbo that is the auctioneer's special language. His deep, mellifluous voice attracts and compels, builds excitement and momentum, a sense of urgency—bid now or it will be too late. He is unconcerned with breathing and pauses only to announce bids. Say "I love Kentucky Thoroughbreds" as fast as you can, over and over again, slurring the words, running out common linguistic sense and intelligible meaning, compressing the sounds to create phonemes unintelligible to the layman, squeezing all the vowels out and purging half the consonants and you are as close or as far away as anyone to the arcane language of the auction. It is a language not of words, but of momentum, salesmanship:

driving, lulling, coaxing, at times exasperating, but always energized and compelling.

The seated audience of buyers and observers has been divided into smaller domains watched over by bid spotters, men in blue blazers one day, green blazers the next, whose job is to look for the bids and relay them to the auctioneer, where they are stuck into his phoneme soup and then flashed up on a neon tote board above the podium. After the 1983 world-record sale of $10.3 million for a single yearling, Keeneland redesigned the board, adding an eighth digit. With one day's sale already completed, the bid board's new digit is still unused.

If no bid is immediately forthcoming, the spotters may implore the audience. They gesture with their hands, pointing at no one in particular, but pointing at everyone. They hold up their fingers in numbers that correspond to the amount of the bid desired. They point their fingers at the audience, impatient with their indecisiveness. Each spotter carries a sales catalogue. At a dramatic point when the bidding seems to be slowing, or he senses hesitation in his territory, he slaps the catalogue with his open hand two or three times, a noise that he hopes will push the undecided, the timid, into action. And at last, when they have coaxed out that bid, they whirl and thrust their hands into the air and yell "Here!" or "Ha!" as if it were the crowning achievement of their lives. Their victory is short-lived, for the auctioneer has simultaneously accepted the bid and raised it to the next level. He is never satisfied.

The bids come in lots of different ways. Some raise their hands and signal the spotter, uncaring that they become immediately known to the audience. Others consider that effrontery and signal by sticking a leg out in the aisle, or nodding their head slightly, a barely perceptible million-dollar nod. Or they wink an eye, or touch their nose. Some remove their glasses, put them on again. The spotter knows his territory. He looks for eye contact—that's where the next bid is and he knows it before the bidder has opened his mouth.

Behind the podium, with their backs to the audience, are three more spotters who watch the crowded paddock through an open glass window. From their perches, they resemble church priests who have been stationed on high to keep watch on the congregation for signs of inattentiveness or sinful behavior. The yearlings are brought in, one at a time, to the sales ring in front of the podium through

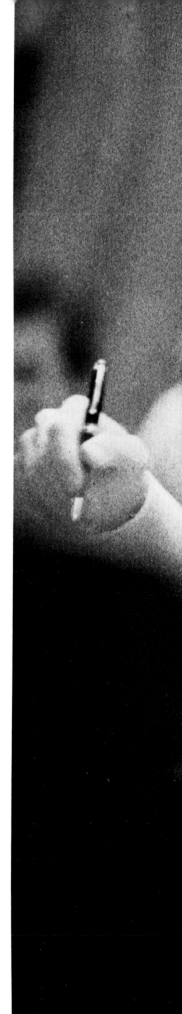

a door that slides open to the left. When a sale is completed, the horse is led out through another sliding door to the right side. The paddock is the staging area, the waiting room, where four or five yearlings at a time are walked to calm them as they await their turn in the auction ring. Many buyers will congregate out in the paddock among the crowd and signal their bids to the spotters. While the bidding proceeds, the horse stands in the sales ring below the elevated podium, held by a gloved groom. The groom jingles the lead chain to calm the horse, but some horses become nervous and will whinny and occasionally rear up or jerk their heads. As soon as the horse has been sold, it is led out, the door no sooner closing than a new horse comes in the other side. The new owner will most likely van his horse to its new home immediately.

Closed-circuit televisions have been placed throughout the stables. Stable hands and passersby gather in front of them to watch the bidding, crying out in unison when their horse reaches a good price, rooting for it to go higher as if they were cheering on their favorite basketball team. For some, the sales are sorrowful times. They have grown attached to the yearlings. A high-school kid with two front teeth missing who gets $3.50 minimum wage working the horses—whether his favorite filly goes for $650,000 or $2.5 million doesn't matter to him. "His" horse is gone, a friend, with a personality, a unique character: "I trained her to wear a cap. She wouldn't walk a lick without a cap on her head."

When bidding on a horse finally stops, and the sale is completed, a Keeneland agent appears within minutes with a sales ticket for the buyer to sign. The buyer is then expected to appear at the sales office within the hour. Buyers who are regular customers at Keeneland establish lines of credit ahead of time and may even deposit sums of money in advance to draw upon. Once the auctioneer strikes the hammer, it's the buyer's horse and "buyer beware" becomes the operable rule. While the stiff entrance requirements minimize the possibility of fraud, there are stories of misinformation and mistakes that have become part of the history of the Keeneland auction. For instance, the owner of a horse must inform the auctioneer if his horse is a "cribber," prone to fasten onto things with his teeth and suck air, a lifelong habit that can lead to real digestive problems for the horse. A cribber must be advertised as such during the sale. Not too long ago, at Keeneland, the auctioneer forgot to post the fact that a certain

horse was a cribber. Bidding reached several million dollars before the owner realized what had happened. He informed the auctioneer, who was required to void the bidding—wipe out a multimillion-dollar sale—and start over again. In that case, the horse was so highly valued regardless that bidding quickly reached the several-million-dollar level again.

The auction goes on through the afternoon. The eighth digit on the tote board remains unlighted. At 4:00, Hip #215 enters the paddock and proceeds toward the sales ring. The crowd suddenly gets larger and noisier in anticipation of what may be the highest price of the sale. The colt is led onto the stage. The announcer reads his pedigree: The colt is by Nijinsky II, out of My Charmer. The pedigree is the bluest of blood. Sire of more than eighty stakes winners, Nijinsky II, a son of Northern Dancer, also a great racehorse and progenitor, is one of the leading breeding stallions of England. Nijinsky's progeny include champions galore: Golden Fleece, champion three-year-old in England and Ireland, Epsom Derby winner; Ile de Bourbon, champion twice in England; Caerleon, French Derby winner; DeLa Rose, with lifetime earnings of $544,647 and winner of the Hollywood Derby; Solford, champion miler in Ireland; Cherry Hinton, in England; Princess Lida, in France, the Prix Morny; and Maruzen Sukih, in Japan. My Charmer is no slouch of a companion. She is dam of five winners, including Seattle Slew, a champion as a two- and three-year-old, winner of fourteen races in seventeen starts, among them the Kentucky Derby and the Triple Crown.

The bidding opens at $1 million. The high figure electrifies the crowd. In rapid order, the bids reach $2 million and then begin escalating in increments of $500,000. At $9.5 million, the pace slows. Three groups remain in the bidding at this point. The eighth digit on the bid board lights up for the first time as the bidding reaches $10 million. One of the groups drops out at $10.1. The bids move quickly from $10.1 to $10.2, tying the world record set in 1983. A nod at the auctioneer breaks the record with $10.3. The auctioneer remarks, ''You ain't seen nothin' yet.'' How high will both groups go for the colt is the question. The bidding slows again as the auctioneer is able to coax only bids of $100,000 as the total rises to $11.5. The two groups are syndicates, one a partnership of foreign and American buyers, who most likely will take the horse to Europe. The other is

entirely American. At $11.5, the ante jumps to $11.7, but a counter bid
raises to $12. The American group holds at $12.3, hears a counter to
$12,350,000, huddles, and raises to $12.4, hoping the purchase price
is near. But again, their opponent raises by $100,000. The Americans
confer hurriedly, then, striking for the prize, jump the bid to $13
million. Again, with scarcely a pause, there is a retaliatory nod to the
auctioneer and the bid rises to $13.1. The Americans confer again.
The auctioneer asks if they "want to try them just one more time."
The Americans shake their heads no and continue to shake them as
the auctioneer says, "Thirteen million, two hundred thousand
anywhere . . . well, thirteen one, then, sold." The audience erupts
into applause and well-wishers swarm over to the buyers. The
Americans settle back into their seats, their arms crossed. The
wooden door to the right of the sales ring slides open and the world's
most expensive yearling leaves as Hip #216 comes into the ring.

By sale's end, nine of Nijinsky's progeny will have sold for
$26,725,000, an average of more than $2.9 million. Another Nijinsky II
colt will be bought for $7 million in the name of Sheikh Maktoum Bin
Rashid al Maktoum. When the final bidding is done, twenty-four
yearlings will have brought $1 million or more and the gross total for
the entire Keeneland sale will be $138,645,000, an average of
$537,383. The consignor who sold the record breaker will sell eight
yearlings altogether for $19,470,000, an average sum of $2,433,750.

The vans are busy from morning to night, loading the horses to
transport them to their homes. When the horses are gone, the
procession of hats will stop. The company will go home in their
pickups and Mercedes and private planes. The farms will turn to the
business of training the yearlings for racing, and preparing for next
year's crop of yearlings. The bright summery days will shorten. The
bluegrass will send forth rhizomes to form new plants that will shoot
up in the fall. By then, and most likely long before, Hip #215 will have
registered a name with The Jockey Club. Only a few, perhaps as
many as six or seven of the yearlings in the sale, will ever win a
stakes race. The dice have been thrown, and only time will tell
whether the son of Nijinsky II, out of My Charmer, a Kentucky-bred
Thoroughbred and the world's only $13.1 million yearling, is one
of the lucky few.

The white plank fences catch the first light of dawn. In the evening, they glow with light long after the trees and pastures have become dark. In the bright midday sun, the fences become frames for the emerald velvet images pressed onto the gently undulating pages of a giant photo album. Kept constantly in good repair, the white fences seem perfect and unchanging. They help to create the mystique of Kentucky horse country.

The fences of the bluegrass are not, however, all white fences. There are dark plank fences, stained rather than painted. These dark fences—though they are not remembered—outnumber the white fences. In this era of extreme practicality, dark fences make more sense—they are less expensive to maintain, and, some say, less self-promoting.

The Bright Pastoral Image

Within the family of plank fences, there are subspecies, each adapted to a specific function. There are three-plank and four-plank fences. Amazingly, there are fences with five planks. Three- and four-plank fences are comprehensible. Three-plank fences are all that are necessary to fence in mature, fully grown horses. A younger horse that lies down to sleep near a three-plank fence might roll under. A fourth plank just above ground level rails him in. A farmer with a three- or four-plank fence does not understand why someone wants yet another board to repair and paint. Five-plank white fences, they say, are for people who want their farms photographed for magazines.

There are fences of limestone rocks cut from nearby quarries that flourished when limestone was a major building material. That was before man understood the effect of moisture on limestone. The quarries are now abandoned and concealed by second- and third-growth forest. But the fences endure. The limestone rocks were carted to the farms and stacked by slaves as anonymous now as the horses they walled in. They topped off their stone fences by stacking slate on end to offer jagged edges to the passing stranger. The edges were a barrier, a gentlemanly reminder to the outside world to respect the privacy and the rights of those inside. Crumbling now in the face of irrevocable chemistry, these limestone walls are monuments to another era.

All of the fences in the bluegrass link the present with the past. They still fence croplands to keep animals out and enclose pastures to keep them in. The business of repairing them still contributes to the local economy. Fences on some of the multithousand-acre farms in the bluegrass can keep a single fence company employed year round. They no sooner finish than it is time to start again. In 1879, it was estimated that two billion rails cut from seventy million prime rail trees were needed to fence Kentucky's 125,000 farms. Annual repairs, if made properly—if done in strict adherence to the state's fencing laws—would have required an additional 280 million rails cut from another ten million trees. Labor and materials were reckoned to cost approximately $75 million, almost seventy times the state appropriations for the support of public education that year.

The fences measure distance and direction in the bluegrass. They guide country roads through early-morning mists. At night, they project the headlights of cars safely through the tunnels made by the

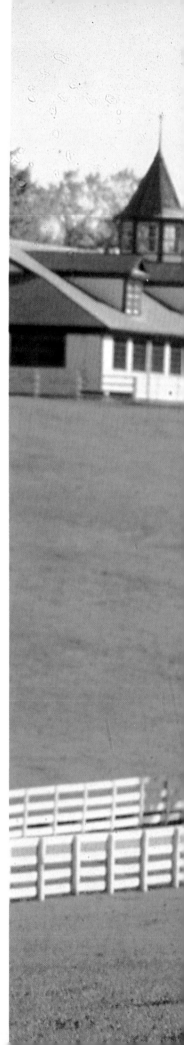

dark canopies of trees along the narrow roads. They protect horses from trees and from each other. The horse's most dangerous natural enemy in the bluegrass is the groundhog. No respecter of fences, he burrows into the root system of trees. His burrowing leaves leg-breaking holes around the circumference of a tree. The fences keep the horses out from under the trees, away from the holes. Double rows of pasture fences make good neighbors of stallions. They cannot get close enough to nip or paw or kick at each other.

The blueness of the grass comes and fades; the mythic, steel-springed horses breed and die; but the fences endure, providing order and stability to the bluegrass country.

In the year 1776, when the thirteen American colonies declared their independence, there was a captain of Virginia militia who owned a 210-acre farm in Rockingham County among the green hills that bordered the Shenandoah Valley. He thought Virginia already crowded, the prospects for fortune and adventure dimmed by the ever-increasing population of the Shenandoah. A friend named Daniel Boone had been exploring land beyond the mountains since 1767. He had returned to tell of lush, hardwood forests, and valleys rich with black soil, of clear, running waters and abundant game and fish. The Indian name for it translated into Kentucky.

The country where land was forty cents an acre beckoned him. In 1782, he sold his farm and, with his wife and family of three sons and two daughters, joined a party heading west. They journeyed down the Wilderness Road, which Boone and a party of thirty men had cut with axes seven years earlier. The trail led down the Shenandoah Valley, across the Cumberland Mountains, through Cumberland Gap into Central Kentucky, where Boone had built a fort called Boonesborough, twenty miles south of where Lexington is today.

Turning north, then west into Kentucky, the militia captain stopped at the Green River, where he filed claim for more than 2,000 acres. A year later, while he worked in his fields, he was shot through the chest with a musketball from an Indian rifle. In time, his sons would live in different places in Kentucky. One of them, Thomas, a migratory carpenter and farmer, resided for a while in Hardin County, now Larue County, eighty-seven miles southwest of Lexington. He took for his wife a local woman named Nancy Hanks. It was their firstborn on

February 12, 1809, whom they named in honor of Thomas' father, Abraham Lincoln. Thomas later moved his family across the Ohio River to settle in Indiana and then in Illinois, where his son taught himself by reading deeply in a small stock of books.

Samuel Davis, on the other hand, left his home in Todd County in south central Kentucky, 137 miles southwest of Lincoln's birthplace, and migrated with his family south—down the Ohio River, beyond where it joins the Mississippi River at Cairo, Illinois, southward to the undeveloped state of Mississippi. He became a cotton planter and a slave owner. He soon had means enough to send his son Jefferson to receive a classical education at Transylvania University in Lexington, and from there, an appointment to West Point, where he graduated in 1828.

Thus did colonial Kentucky supply the new country the two leaders of the opposing sides in the Civil War, enhancing its own already considerable mystique, at the same time that it further confused its identity.

Just as it inspired the grandfather of Abraham Lincoln, Boone's trailblazing in Kentucky helped fuel an immense land fever in the East during the last twenty-five years of the 18th century. The emigrants invaded Boone's Kentucky, as many as 20,000 in a year. They came along the Ohio River or, in larger numbers, through the Cumberland Gap. In 1792, Kentucky entered the Union as the Commonwealth of Kentucky, the fifteenth state and the first state west of the Appalachians. By the end of the century, Kentucky had attracted 220,000 settlers and had the sixth largest population among the states.

The earliest travelers wrote glowingly of the "transmontane garden" that "stuck like an arrow into the West." The fertile, promising land, which "in the profusion of her bounty, had spread a feast for all that lives, both for the animal and rational world," stirred those who saw her "to want to kiss her soil in imitation of Columbus as he hailed and saluted the sand on his first setting foot on the shores of America"—so wrote Felix Walker, in mid-March 1775. He was a North Carolinian, a member of an advance party of the Transylvania Company, whose members, including Boone, were cutting a trail through the woods of eastern Kentucky.

"This country is more temperate and healthy than the other settled parts of America. In summer, it wants the sandy heats of Virginia and

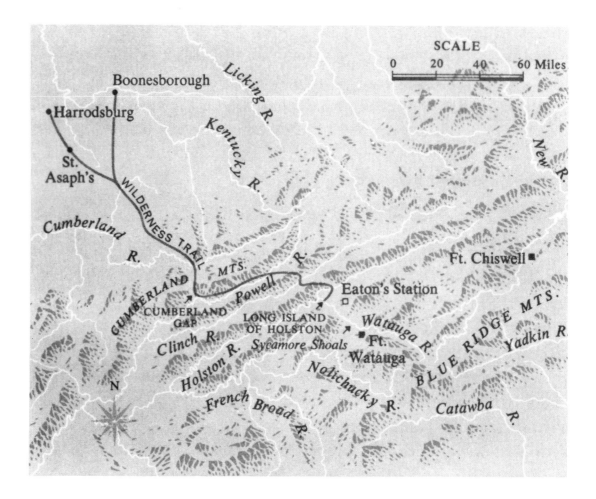

Carolina experience, and receives a fine air from its rivers. Winter
at most lasts 3 months, usually two, and is seldom severe. One may
view . . . the most extraordinary country upon which the sun ever
shone.'' (A Topographical Description of the Western Country of North
America by Gilbert Imlay, 1792.)

The earliest arrivals saw immense, rolling savannahs covered with
deep, dark, loose soil that grew abundant wild lettuce, pepper-grass,
wild rye, clover, buffalo grass, and wildcane that provided excellent
feed for livestock. The profusion of wild herbs and flowers added
to its paradisiacal quality. The forests offered equal bounty: sugar
trees, buckeye, white walnut, the papaw, the coffee, and the white
and black and blue ash. There was honey locust surrounded by large
thorny spikes that bore broad and long pods in the form of sweet-
tasting peas, which made excellent beer, and cherry trees whose

Daniel Boone

boards were good lumber. Though he would come much later to the forests, John Muir, on his 1,000-mile walk to the Gulf, which took him into Kentucky in September of 1867, wrote, "I have seen oaks of many species and kind . . . but those in Kentucky excel in grandeur all that I ever before had beheld. They are broad and dense and bright green. In the leafy bowers and caves of their long branches dwell magnificent avenues of shade and every tree seems to be blessed with a double portion of strong exulting life."

The pioneers settled first in the bluegrass area, where the richest land was. A census taken between 1790 and 1795 shows all Kentucky towns were within or on the margin of the bluegrass, within easy access to springs and salt licks. The land was relatively even and easy to clear. The richness of the soil and the pasture soon gave rise to stories of amazing fecundity, stories that drifted over the mountains —of ground that produced 100 bushels of corn per acre, of soil favorable to flax, hemp, turnips, potatoes, tobacco, "soil that every husbandman might have a good garden or meadow without water, or manure [Imlay]." By the end of the 1700s, bluegrass farms were dotted with good-grade livestock. Local markets burst with hempen shocks, hogsheads of tobacco, and cured meats. The image of Kentucky as a bright pastoral land full of "exulting life" had become quickly and firmly fixed for posterity.

This bright pastoral land had once been covered by an ocean of two waters. The northern waters extended down from what is now the Hudson Bay. The southern waters came from the Gulf of Mexico. The oceans began to recede and, as they did, tremendous shifting in the sediment occurred, caused by folding and faulting. The Upper Carboniferous period, 280 million years ago, was the formative era for the topography of modern Kentucky. The great ice sheets that intermittently moved down from the north across the North American continent during the Pleistocene epoch, which began two million years ago and ended with the last glacial period 11,000 years ago, left Kentucky relatively undisturbed. When the glaciers approached Kentucky, the climate seemed to change for the warmer, arresting their movement just south of what is now the Ohio River.

To the Carboniferous period, sixty-five million years long, does modern Kentucky owe its reputation as the leading producer of coal in the United States. The plant life that abounded in that time

fossilized and formed two vast coal regions in Kentucky. One was in the west, an extension of the central interior coal field of southern Illinois and Indiana; the other was the Cumberland Plateau on the margin of the great Appalachian field represented in western Virginia and Pennsylvania.

The region between the two coal fields was folded and uplifted continuously, leaving a plateau that today slopes from an altitude of 1,050 feet in the southeast to 900 feet at Cincinnati to 800 feet and less to the northwest. Geologists named this slightly upraised area "the Cincinnati Arch." It came to be known more popularly as the bluegrass region. It is a region of rolling upland country, surrounded

by a belt of isolated hills that have been detached from one another by erosion and are known as knobs. Underneath the arch are older formations of massive, pure limestone. Limestone outcrops on almost every road in Fayette County, and has figured prominently throughout the history of the state. Plantation homes were once built of limestone blocks and slabs. Soft, coarse crystalline limestone was crushed and used to top roads. Frost and rain caused rapid deterioration and limestone was soon replaced by more resistant building materials.

Through the ages, rivers and springs in the bluegrass have trenched themselves to depths of 400–500 feet, washing out miles of subterranean passages and gorging themselves at places like High Bridge and Jessamine County south of Lexington, where the Kentucky River has carved out limestone bluffs that tower 300 feet. The Kentucky and the Ohio rivers are among the most erratic-coursed rivers in the waterways of the continent. All of the rivers of Kentucky, unlike the rivers of its eastern neighbors, drain to the west.

The gently rolling topography and the rigid channels of water flow have held erosion in the bluegrass region to a minimum. A deep, dark-brown limestone soil rich in phosphorus and calcium, and well drained by a profusion of sinkholes, has eroded evenly and deeply over this inner plateau. It is known as Maury silt loam. When Kentuckians are asked to explain what makes Kentucky horses so special, they answer without pause that it's the Maury soil—it makes good pasture and gives the horses calcium for strong bones.

While ice sheets covered the land north of the Ohio River, Kentucky teemed with animals. Their bones have been dug up by the tons from the marshes and swamps around the salt licks where the animals perished and where their bones were trampled into the soft soil. In 1795, General William Henry Harrison filled wagons full of mastodon teeth from Big Bone Lick near Covington, Kentucky. Since then, Big Bone Lick has supplied the world with Pleistocene mammal material. Toward the end of the last glacial period, primitive man appeared in Kentucky. He was late, after the horse.

The horse had already appeared . . . and disappeared . . . from the North American continent. The Kentucky Thoroughbred and all horses trace their lineage to a small, puny-looking animal, Eohippus, for whom paleontologists have identified some 200 species in about nineteen genera. Eohippus, or Hyracotherium as he is also known, means shrew beast. The ancient relative lived sixty million years ago on the North American continent during the Eocene epoch. Skeletal remains suggest an animal with a long pointed nose, narrow piglike eyes, and a stooped neck, an animal the size of a fox terrier, about twelve inches high. Its hindquarters are thought to have resembled those of a jackrabbit, its head, that of a sheep. It had multiple toes, four on each forefoot, three on each hind foot, and low crowned teeth for feeding on leaves and fronds. The Eocene earth was soft and swampy, which made multiple-toed feet an advantage. The large size of its legs suggest fleetness. That quality, along with its ability to breed prolifically, ensured both its survival and its spread across the Northern Hemisphere. It crossed the land bridge to North America, in reverse direction from the mastodons, migrating to Asia, continental Europe, and the British Isles.

By the time of the Oligocene epoch, thirty-eight to twenty-six million years ago, the horse had grown larger, the size of a sheep. As climates changed, it extended its neck for grazing on the grasses that

prevailed. The front feet consolidated to three toes, the middle one of which was more prominent than the others. It appears that the animal ran only on the middle toe, and this adaptation may have occurred because of the harder surfaces on the huge tracts of plains that followed the forests.

The horse evolved further as a grazer during the Miocene epoch, twenty-six to twelve million years ago. It stood about four feet high and had a fully developed hoof to withstand the hard surfaces of its habitat on the plains. Its teeth had become harder, higher crowned. The enamel was covered with cement to withstand the wear and tear of the silica in the stems and seeds of the grasses and the sand and dirt that grazers grind up.

The horse had assumed its modern characteristics by the Pleistocene epoch, when, for reasons unknown, it disappeared from the North American continent. It is thought, inconclusively, that the arrival of migrant hunters from Asia may have caused their demise. Remnants of the early horse are included among the fossils found at Big Bone Lick, but there are no fossils of modern horse, and the period from about 7000 B.C. to the 16th century remains devoid of horses on this continent.

It was Christopher Columbus who reintroduced horses to the New World. As he prepared to depart for his second voyage to America, he hoisted twenty horses aboard his ship. They were intended to be superior Arabian mounts first introduced to Spain by the Arabs and prized for their strength and endurance. However, at the last minute, his men traded them for cheap plugs and pocketed the profit, not the last time horses would figure unpredictably in the economy of the New World. The civilized world was, of course, totally dependent on the horse by the time of the discovery of America. But it was apparently the first sea voyage of such length for horses. Records show that William the Conqueror ferried horses across the English Channel in 1066 on specially constructed scows to battle the Saxons, and that crusaders transported horses to Palestine, but no such long sea voyage had been attempted before. Columbus' horses survived the crossing. When he arrived in Hispaniola, now Haiti and the Dominican Republic, there was no way to offload the horses except by pushing them overboard to swim to shore.

The horses were the precursors of the breeding ranches that developed in the West Indies and supplied the animals used by the

Spanish expeditionary forces in their conquest of Mexico and South America, and, in time, by the American colonists. (The term *horse latitudes*—which describes two belts of latitude where winds are light and the weather is hot and dry, located mostly over the oceans at about thirty degrees latitude in each hemisphere, with a north-south range of about five degrees—supposedly derives from the days when Spanish sailing ships transporting horses to the West Indies would become becalmed in mid-ocean in this latitude. The resulting prolongation of the voyage caused water shortages and would force the crews to throw their horses overboard.)

Driven by their search for gold in the New World, the Spaniards parlayed a minuscule number of horses into overwhelming military advantage over the Indians they encountered. Cortes' initial expeditionary force into Mexico in 1519 consisted of 500 men and just sixteen horses, obtained from Cuba, progeny no doubt of the stock brought by Columbus to Hispaniola. In one of his early encounters with the Indians, Cortes flanked his adversaries with a band of thirteen armed caballeros. While his main body of foot soliders battled the thousands of enemy on a wide savannah, his cavalry circled to the rear and struck at them from behind: "As the plain was bare and the horsemen were good riders, and some of the horses were very swift and nimble, they came quickly upon them and speared them as they chose. Caught between the horsemen and the soldiers, the Indians turned tail. They had never seen a horse before and they thought the horse and rider were one creature," wrote Bernal Diaz, one of Cortes' soldiers who kept a journal of the conquest of Mexico.

The Spaniards sealed the wounds of their horses with fat from the corpse of an Indian they had cut up, and marched on. When a delegation of Indians offered to negotiate a peace with the Spaniards, Cortes exploited their fear of the horses. He led a mare in heat to the area where the peace negotiations would occur long enough for the mare to leave her scent. He then removed her from sight. He brought in the randiest of his stallions to scent the mare. He then tethered the stallion near the spot of the peace negotiations. When the Indians arrived, Cortes expressed his displeasure with their hostile actions. He warned them to behave peacefully in the future, or else. At this point, he gave a secret sign to fire a cannon. Its thunderous report thoroughly terrified the Indians. Cortes next brought in the stallion and tethered it where it could again catch the scent of the mare from the ground where it had stood and which happened to be occupied now by the Indians. The stallion began to paw the ground and neigh and create an uproar, looking all the time toward the Indians, who thought the stallion was roaring at them and became even more terrified.

In the subsequent conquest of Peru and Bolivia, and the exploration and settlement of the American Southwest —as far north as Kansas, and west to California—the horse was again a featured player. Not only in military encounters, but in the mining and transporting of gold and silver to the seacoasts for transport back to Spain, and in herding cattle on the vast ranches the conquerors established. It was the long trains of mules and horses packed with precious metals that first attracted the attention of marauders like Sir Francis Drake. He crossed and recrossed the Isthmus of Panama in 1572 to capture three mule trains bearing thirty tons of silver.

Neither mules nor horses had an easy job of it. The horses in the mines were used brutally as a source of power and discarded as soon as they wore out. They pulled the ore from the depths of the mines and dragged the heavy stones that crushed the ore to a fine powder. To get a heavier concentration of ore, the ground ore was mixed with quicksilver, then the quicksilver was distilled, leaving the ore. To get a good mix, the thick mud of ore and quicksilver was spread the depth of a foot or two on a hard surface such as a courtyard, surrounded by walls or some enclosure. The Spaniards then herded wild horses into the courtyard and drove them to a frenzy by waving blankets and lashing them with whips. The horses' hooves churned the mud thoroughly. At the same time, the abrasion of the "mud" wore away the hair, hide, and flesh just above the hooves, ruining the animals. They were then taken out and slaughtered, their meat used to feed the miners who were often Indians, and their hides used for leather. The well-ground mud was carefully gathered up and washed in a sluice to separate the heavy amalgam from the lighter waste material.

The Spaniards needed horses for their haciendas and cattle ranches. They trained Indians to ride them to work the cattle. A hard-riding cowhand might use seven or eight horses for range work at round-up time, as well as two or three trained roping and cutting horses for branding. A cowhand's horse needed about three days' grazing to recuperate from a day's work, especially if the riding were over hard, rocky ground. In that case, the horse might need additional

days to allow its hooves to heal, since very few of them were shod. And very few were fed on grain; most had to subsist on grazing.

Indian attacks on the Spaniards, thievery, and inadequate fencing resulted in the escape of horses into the wilderness. They bred to become wild mustangs and the other wild horses of the American West. The diffusion of horses across 16th-century America spreads north out of Mexico, branches eastward from Mexico around 1600, and meanders across the Mississippi, where it splits, one fork moving along the Arkansas River into Tennessee, northward into Kentucky, where it parallels another line that emanates from a different source, St. Augustine in Florida. The ranches of the West Indies had become the first great purveyors of horses for the New World. The ranchers constructed ship-deck pens for the animals and sent as many as 200 at a time to the American mainland to colonists who found it much cheaper to import stock that way than across the ocean from Europe. The West Indians found the trade extremely profitable.

For much of the 17th century in colonial America, and especially in the northeastern colonies, horses were regarded mainly as work animals. It was a period in the history of this country when there was little time and resource for leisure activities. Nor were horses as highly valued as oxen. Oxen could produce milk, meat, hides, and tallow in addition to serving as beasts of burden. Horses required more upkeep—grain or hay in the winter to supplement their feed. Increasing emigration pushed settlement farther westward, and increased need for transportation increased the need for more horses. Farmers discovered that the horse was more nimble and maneuverable, its gait twice as speedy as the oxen's. The steady gait of a horse was more feasible for pulling the new machines designed to operate at a constant speed, such as the reaper invented in 1831.

Whereas the conquistadors had brought a war horse, the colonists used horses to pull stumps and plow fields and for transportation. Lacking the vast open ranges of the West, the colonists quartered their horses on small farms in ones and twos. Again, Indian encounters, thievery, and inadequate fencing resulted in horses escaping into the wilderness, or else living in semi-feral conditions. On occasion, Indians would pen the horses in corrals and slaughter them with arrows, cutting off their tails as trophies. Laws were formulated that allowed farmers to shoot with impunity any free-ranging horse that came into his field or orchard for the third time.

Not surprisingly, the Northeast with its crowded land and small farms preferred docile, sturdy workhorses. Stallions were often hard to tame and dangerous to have on a small farm. Thus, in a farming community, a business might be made of supplying the stallion service for the area. Like an itinerant schoolteacher, the stallion's owner would travel around the country with his stallion during breeding season to offer his services. He could charge $15 to $20 for the covering of a mare. Stallions who sired superior foals were in constant demand at a good fee. Breeding sheds, as they were, and stables were open chinked loghouses or barns, or, tobacco sheds.

Young stallions were often gelded before they were sold to eastern farms, since it was not considered desirable to breed them to get good workhorses. In fact, only geldings and mares were wanted in the eastern markets. The popular western stallions with the legacy of the Spanish horses were considered good range horses because they were strong, tough, and hardy, but were thought too small and light to be draft horses or even good riding horses. By the same token, the mares of Spanish stock, when they were crossed with larger stallions, produced good foals that grew much larger than their dams, partly because of the heritage of their sires, partly because they had good pastures and supplemental feed during the growing period and were not subjected to the harsher environment of the open range.

In the South, the horse fared differently. The 120 colonists who landed at Jamestown in 1609 brought with them six mares and two stallions but were forced to eat them for lack of food. The development of farms and plantations, however, in particular the tobacco plantations, required horses and mules. The wealthy landowners and merchants owned a large number of fine horses for pleasure riding and driving, for fox hunting and for racing. The overseers preferred light, easier-to-maneuver horses to ride, and came to value saddlehorses, as they were called. They paid little attention to the draft horses. Consequently, the proportion of fine riding horses in the total horse population was high, especially in the towns and around the larger plantations. They, too, were beset with familiar problems: Horses escaped and roamed areas like the Blue Ridge Mountains, grazing and ruining farms. Virginia passed laws to require fencing and tethering of stallions and mares.

When the colonists of the Carolinas and Georgia during the 18th century came into contact with the Indians, they found them riding

small, fine steeds measuring thirteen hands. The Indian tribes who rode them—the Chickasaw, Choctaw, and Cherokees—seemed expert in their knowledge of them and practiced in the art of breeding for purity in their stock. The colonists admired them and in time acquired and bred them for their own use, producing strong, fast, and beautiful colts.

On June 4, 1775, some hunters camping near a spring in the bluegrass, which was crossed and crisscrossed by trails, heard news of the Battle of Lexington that had occurred two months earlier on April 19, marking the opening engagement of the American Revolution. They decided to commemorate the battle by naming their hunting camp Lexington. The county in which Lexington was founded, Fluvanna, was the centerpiece in the bluegrass region. Located in a great bend of the Kentucky River, fifteen miles distant, along a branch of the Elkhorn Creek, the town grew astride major avenues of migration for buffaloes, Indians, and, in time, traders passing to and from the Ohio River. An early map shows fifteen roads coming to confluence at the intersection of where Broadway, Limestone, and Main streets are today.

Lexington built its prosperity on agricultural products. Hemp, a rough fiber that provided sturdy cordage and a rough cloth for rope and sails, grew easily and richly in the Maury soil. The invention of the cotton gin in 1793 made possible larger-volume production of cordage and bagging for cotton bales and for sailcloth for the ever-increasing trade on the Ohio River. Hemp helped Lexington become the major western supply depot for the fiber. Its seeds and fibers were even used as money among the cash-poor farms.

By the 1780s, bluegrass farmers were harvesting crops of loose-leaf tobacco. When the port of New Orleans was opened in 1789, tobacco began to move out of the country to eastern and European markets in larger quantities. As early as the 1790s, Kentucky tobacco was highly prized. By the Civil War, Kentucky smokes and chews were considered premier. The state grew the largest amount of tobacco in the country until 1929, when North Carolina surpassed it. Kentucky today ranks second in total production of burley tobacco.

The rich farmland produced a variety of rich grains, which in turn led to the creation of some powerful concoctions—immense quantities of alcoholic beverages, large quantities of cider and peach brandy.

Mash from surplus corn yielded excellent quantities of distilled spirits and before long, that "uniquely mellow and delicious cornliquor" known as bourbon was created. The quality of the bourbon was attributed to the limestone spring water. The state soon developed a national reputation for its bourbon. Today, more than two-thirds of all American whiskey is manufactured in Kentucky. Bourbon has been recognized by the U.S. Congress as one of our distinctive national products.

The raising of horses and livestock completed the basis of Lexington's economic as well as its social and cultural life. From the very beginning, the bluegrass became renowned for its livestock. The settlers in the region brought with them their cows, pigs, sheep, and horses. So natural a role did horses play in the settlement of Kentucky, that like the early pioneers, they blend without distinction into the history of colonial Kentucky. In *Agrarian Kentucky* (p. 32), historian Thomas D. Clark writes:

No long-suffering pioneer came into the new land and endured greater hardships than did those plodding animals who bore burdensome packs westward. They trod treacherous trails across mountainous wilderness, forded flooded streams, and even faced marauding wild parties of Indians. They came into the land without distinction of blooded ancestry or assurances of posterity, but these patient beasts bore the material trappings of Anglo-American civilization. Most important of all, these trail horses transported a small army of women and children to make new beginnings in virgin country.

This seems like an appropriate place to digress on the subject of what these valiant beasts of burden found by way of pasture when they arrived in places like Kentucky. There is some controversy about the origin of bluegrass. Some believe it was here when the first settlers arrived; others think the early settlers of Kentucky brought with them seeds of a particular strain of grass from the Old World, a species of range and pasture grass that grew well in temperate and cool regions. In either event, of the large and widely distributed genus *Poa*, bluegrass is any of several different species. One of the best known and most important varieties is the sod-forming Kentucky bluegrass or June grass (*Poa pratensis*). (A sod is the density of plants per square foot.) Kentucky became known as the bluegrass state

because the species grew to be so prevalent, especially as the early farmers increased the amount of open land by clearing the thick forests that Boone had encountered. Kentucky bluegrass today is also found next door in Tennessee, Missouri, Kansas, Nebraska, and all over the United States and Canada. In general, bluegrasses are perennial, with fine-leaved foliage that is bluish green in some species. Specifically, *Poa pratensis* has a bluish cast for two or three days in May as a result of the color in the outer glumes of the anthers in the flowers. Bluegrass has a rhizome that spreads out from the plant and in this manner propagates itself. It forms its underground stems in July and August. In the fall, from October through December, the stems turn up and form additional plants. In drought, the grass will dry up and look dead, but with the first rain, it bounces right back. Grazing causes the grass to propagate better, to make better sods. The underground roots help to make good sod or turf. The grass has a better protein level if it is kept clipped. The longer it grows, the more lignified it becomes, meaning the component of fiber increases, making the grass less digestible if it has too much fiber.

By 1814, Lexington had become the economic, social, and cultural capital of the new country, not to mention its largest and wealthiest city. Described as the Athens of the West, as the Philadelphia of Kentucky, it had the oldest university west of the Alleghenies, Transylvania, chartered in 1780. The city's prosperous merchants had invested their surplus money in land and country estates, constructing lavish rural retreats that became famous for their charm and conviviality. Some fifty or sixty villas, on a scale with those in the French chateau country, dotted the countryside around Lexington. The city had an air of leisure and opulence, ease and politeness that evinced the cultivation of taste and good feeling. Their balls and assemblies were conducted with as much grace and ease as the best in Europe, and the dresses at the parties were as tasteful and elegant. Even the taverns were different! They seemed to be much more genteel than those of Atlantic towns. They were populated by assemblies of great and well-dressed boarders, townsmen and strangers alike. Meals were served with no small degree of display and splendor, with a hostess usually conducted by some dandy to her chair at the head of the table. The people themselves were, in general, the largest race that Timothy Flint, an early traveler to Kentucky, had ever seen:

*You will nowhere see fairer and fresher complexions, or fuller and
finer forms, than you see in the young men and women of Kentucky.
Such people lived easily and plentifully and on the finest of the wheat.*

The ease and opulence so visible in the appearance of the people
was equally so in their houses and furniture. No wonder that
Kentuckians seemed to glow in complexion with contentedness, that
Kentucky became synonymous in so many minds with all that is
good, fertile, happy, and great. A Methodist preacher capped his
sermon one Sunday by saying, "My brethren, to say all in one word,
heaven is a Kentuck of a place." Such praise, even if self-generated,
added greatly to the mystique of the region, to the association of life
in the bluegrass with paradise.

Many settlers who had entered this paradise from Virginia had
brought with them the offspring of Virginia horses, which were
considered then to be the finest saddlehorses. Early travelers

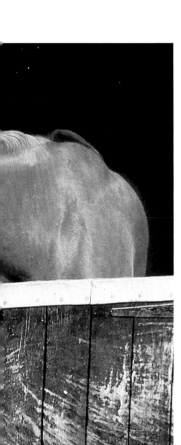

to Kentucky often remarked on the number and the quality of Kentucky horses. Almost all the inhabitants of the state seemed to employ themselves in training and meliorating the breed of horses. The bluegrass region in particular seemed to grow strong, much-admired horses. Farmers of the bluegrass had discovered that feeding their horses on Indian corn provided twice the nutritional value of oats. A visitor to Lexington in 1806 noted a high number of horses tethered around the market. Lexington's population in 1806 was 3,000, including 1,165 blacks. The citizens of Lexington owned a total of 1,500 "good and valuable" horses. As proof of how far luxury had progressed—and of the equation of fine horses with luxury—one observer counted thirty-nine two-wheel carriages and twenty-one four-wheel coaches. A taste for show and expense already pervaded the country, along with talk of bloodlines and newly imported English stud horses. Horses seemed to be the favorite and universal amusement throughout the area. Strangers thought nothing of inviting other strangers to swap horses.

As a further digression, it must be noted that the business of horse swapping gave rise to finagling and crookedness that made horse trading, universally, the same chancy business that used-car trading is today. There was little the unscrupulous would not do to hide the defects of the beasts they were trying to unload: A dose of cocaine rubbed on a horse's tongue could bring to life even the most tired of nags. It created a high that usually lasted long enough for the seller to skip town. A skinny piece of horseflesh could be temporarily fattened up by rubbing its tongue with arsenic, which caused water from the horse's body to gather under the skin, giving it a plump, if not squishy look. A bull windy, a horse with a larynx condition that caused loud, violent breathing and general debilitation, could be disguised by plugging its nostrils with lemon halves shoved far enough up out of sight of the buyer. As the lemons shrunk over time, they would slip down, or the horse when exerted would sneeze and blow them out. Sponges served just as well. Pebbles dropped into the ears of a balky, slow-moving, reluctant horse would get the horse prancing and shaking its head as if it were a fiery steed raring to go. By the same token, wads of cotton soaked in chloroform and jammed up the horse's nostrils just before bargaining could calm an overzealous, cantankerous horse. Cribbers could be doctored by sawing between the incisor teeth or driving small wedges into the teeth, or by cutting and burning the gums—all to make the mouth sore and the horse reluctant to grab onto anything. And a horse could be made to look like a workhorse by rubbing a little croton oil on the hair to make creases that resembled harness marks. Tooth cups could be recut with acid to mislead, and even a missing tail was replaced on occasion with a false one.

The stallions from Virginia, and in time from England, sired offspring with slim legs and well-proportioned heads, animals that were handsome, strong-legged, and fast. As roads were laid out, horse racing became a popular and rowdy pastime. The development of horse racing in America merits a chapter of its own later, but suffice it to say that at this juncture in early America, the distinction begins to be made between horses as work animals and those bred for sport.

By 1840, there were more than half a million people in Kentucky and the horse population numbered 431,000. Well before the Civil War, Kentucky horses seemed to have been acclaimed widely beyond its borders, especially in the South. The state had become an important supplier of top-quality horses, sending them in droves of fifteen to thirty to the southern states, especially South Carolina. The journey to South Carolina was undertaken in early winter—after the season of the dreaded scourge of the low countries, yellow fever, had passed. The trip of 700 miles took eighteen to twenty days and added 25 to 30 percent to the price of the horses. A fine saddlehorse sold for as much as $140.

The Civil War was the last major war in which the horse played a prominent role. Like other border states, Kentucky was torn by conflict over the slavery issue, and at the outbreak of the war attempted to remain neutral. Confederate forces, however, led by a native son, Albert S. Johnston, invaded and occupied part of southern Kentucky, including Columbus and Bowling Green. In September of 1861, the state legislature voted to oust the Confederates. Ulysses S. Grant crossed the Ohio and took Paducah, forcing Johnston to abandon his Kentucky positions and securing the state for the Union. After a handful of battles in 1862, there was no further major fighting within the state, although Confederate cavalrymen like John Hunt Morgan occasionally led raids into the state, and guerrilla warfare was constant. For Kentucky it was truly a civil war, however. Neighbors, friends, and even families became bitterly divided in their loyalties. Over 30,000 Kentuckians fought for the Confederacy, while about

64,000 fought for the Union. Throughout the conflict, the state supplied horses to northern and southern armies alike.

Morgan had been a manufacturer of hemp, a prominent citizen from a prominent family whose home in downtown Lexington remains today. In 1862–63, Morgan destroyed sixty miles of the Louisville and Nashville Railroad, the supply line of the federal army in Tennessee. He captured 1,900 prisoners, and numerous horses and military stores. His exploits, along with those of his comrades James Ewell Brown and Nathan Bedford Forrest, who also executed a series of brilliant cavalry raids in Kentucky, fired the imagination and further embellished the notion of Kentucky horses as superior. In reality, cavalry were a minuscule number of the vast number of horses used in the war. By far the larger number were draft horses used for hauling guns, ammunition, supplies, food, clothing, camp gear, and wounded men. The North had almost twice the number of horses and mules, some 4½ million to 2.87 million, an advantage that increased greatly as the war went on and southern suppliers like Texas, Arkansas, and Missouri were cut off from the main southern armies. The Civil War marked the zenith of the use in wartime of large masses of cavalry. At the conclusion of the war, Kentucky entered a period of growth and change and bitter turmoil.

Many years earlier, in 1815, a steamboat named *The Enterprise* had become the first steamboat to journey up the Ohio River. Lexingtonians had greeted the news with great enthusiasm, but they had missed the true significance of the event. It was the start of a fundamental change in transportation, a revolution that transformed the economy and the urban prospects for Lexington and the entire state, including the then-struggling little town of Louisville, situated at the Falls of the Ohio. Within three years, trade had begun to bypass the Philadelphia of Kentucky for the faster river route. Prospects for the city declined rapidly, relegating the city to secondary economic status.

As the Industrial Revolution in America accelerated, the horse was rapidly succeeded by the machine. As the role of the workhorse began to diminish, the role of the sport horse began to increase. Northern business and investment looking for opportunities in the South were attracted to Kentucky and elsewhere and quickly reestablished their prewar practices of supporting racing interests and the selected breeding that followed.

It doesn't matter who rides them; it doesn't matter who trains them; and it certainly doesn't matter who owns them. In the end, they will run as fast as they have been bred to run. —Olin Gentry, trainer of five Kentucky Derby winners.

Kentucky-bred horses differ from other horses. They look stronger, healthier. They win more. They owe their difference and superiority not to their descent from a single pair of godlike parents, but to the continued care in selecting and breeding many individuals over many generations.

    Whether for work or play, Americans, and before them the English, the Europeans, the Arabs, and the nomadic tribes of Asia,

Breeding to Win

GAINESWAY SIRE LINES

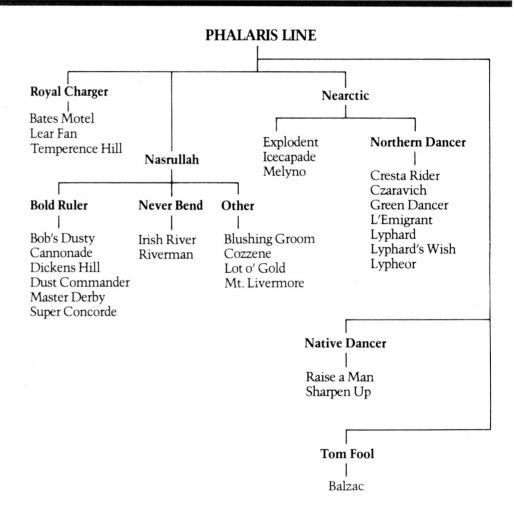

PHALARIS LINE

Royal Charger

Bates Motel
Lear Fan
Temperence Hill

Nasrullah

Bold Ruler

Bob's Dusty
Cannonade
Dickens Hill
Dust Commander
Master Derby
Super Concorde

Never Bend

Irish River
Riverman

Other

Blushing Groom
Cozzene
Lot o' Gold
Mt. Livermore

Nearctic

Explodent
Icecapade
Melyno

Northern Dancer

Cresta Rider
Czaravich
Green Dancer
L'Emigrant
Lyphard
Lyphard's Wish
Lypheor

Native Dancer

Raise a Man
Sharpen Up

Tom Fool

Balzac

have long appreciated fine-quality horses and have tried to perpetuate
the qualities they prized most in breeding their horses. One of the first
laws passed by the first legislative body west of the Alleghenies, the
Boonesborough Assembly, in 1792, dealt with the care and breeding
of quality stock horses.

In the past ten years, in this country and abroad, breeding has
emerged as the big money-maker in the horse business. A champion
like Affirmed, the 1978 Triple Crown winner, was syndicated for
breeding for $22 million. Halo, a stakes winner in his own right, was
the leading sire in North America in 1983 and has sired earners

of more than $1 million for five straight years. He was syndicated for
$36 million. In a sport where an unproven, unnamed yearling can be
sold for $13.1 million, the lure of big money in breeding is
understandable. There is more money to be made in stud fees and
the matching of bloodstock than in winning races. Breeders influence
decisions more and more about the future of successful racers. Often,
a young champion is prematurely retired to take advantage of the
horse's currency as a top-dollar breeding prospect.

Although we are concerned almost exclusively with the
Thoroughbred, the bluegrass country is excellent for all breeds
of horses. The standardbred nurseries in Kentucky rank at the top
in production of trotters and pacers. Harness racing is an outgrowth
of the colonial era, when roads were improved enough to allow light
carriage travel, and to allow the owners of carriages to test the quality
of their rigs and horses against one another's. Kentucky is also the
home of the American saddlebred. When horseback was the principal
means of long-distance travel, people preferred a horse whose gait
minimized the jouncing and thumping of the roads. Horses who
naturally moved by alternately lifting the two feet on one side
together, a more comfortable gait than a trot, were bred to horses with
easy, ambling lateral gaits. In time, they produced horses with easy
gaits used for show and for general riding. Show horses today are
taught to prance, and their tails are formed by clipping the tendons
and shaping them to stand straight and high. For the past several
years, owners of quarterhorses and Arabian breeders have been
investing millions in Kentucky breeding operations. The American
quarterhorse was America's original racehorse, able to sustain a burst
of speed for a few hundred yards, the length of most races in early
America. Still, it is the Kentucky-bred Thoroughbred that gives the
state its prominence in the world of horses.

The Thoroughbred is, in one sense, an invention, one created
by man for speed, for sport. Technically, a horse may look and act
like a Thoroughbred but it is not a Thoroughbred unless its pedigree
authentically traces in all lines to horses recorded in *The American
Stud Book* or a foreign stud book recognized by The Jockey Club and
the International Stud Book Committee. No horse foaled in the United
States or Canada may be registered unless both its sire and dam have
been previously registered in *The American Stud Book*. The rules
further stipulate that Thoroughbred breeding may only occur naturally

and not through embryo transplant or artificial insemination, such as is the case, for instance, in the breeding of Arabian horses.

As a practical matter, the modern Thoroughbred's ancestry can be traced in the direct male line to three eastern horses imported into England at the turn of the 17th century: Byerly Turk, the Godolphin Barb, and the most celebrated of all, Darley Arabian. Arab and Barb horses had first been imported into England fourteen centuries earlier. They were prized for their qualities of stamina, intelligence, and character, as well as their strong legs, and were used to improve the native stock. The Arab was a small, fast horse of about 1,000 pounds,

averaging an inch or two over fourteen hands. The Norman invasion
of England by William the Conqueror and the Crusades provided
further opportunities for crossbreeding. During the age of knighthood
and chivalry, the military preferred horses of stature, large and strong
enough to carry armored soldiers and to wear suits of armor plate
themselves. In an effort to encourage the raising of large horses to suit
the military's needs, Henry VIII (1509–47) forbade the grazing
of horses smaller than fifteen hands on public lands. Eventually,
gunpowder and guns made armor obsolete. The military began
to favor a faster, more agile horse for cavalry. The impetus provided

by military need and demand was matched to some extent by the ascendancy of interest in racing as a sport.

The Stuart monarchs in the 17th century devoted royal attention to racing horses and to breeding imported eastern horses with English breeds. King James made special efforts to improve the breed by importing horses like Markham's Arabian, for which he paid 500 pounds (though the horse never succeeded as a runner). The Lord Protector, Oliver Cromwell, had a breeding stud and owned a celebrated stallion named Place's White Turk. Charles II, who succeeded to the throne upon the restoration of the Stuarts in 1660, established a stud of imported mares that became famous as the "Royal Mares." A record was begun, called *The General Stud Book*, in which are inscribed only those horses that can be traced back to the Royal Mares in direct line, or to the three horses mentioned above.

Byerly Turk arrived in England in 1689, having previously been ridden in warfare by a captain Byerly. The Godolphin Barb arrived in England in 1730. Originally a present to King Louis XIV of France from the Emperor of Morocco, he had come into the possession of a coffee-house owner in London who supposedly had discovered him pulling a cart in Paris. The horse passed eventually into the stud of Lord Godolphin. The Darley Arabian reached England after 1700, sent by a Mr. Darley, who was residing out of the country, to his brother in Yorkshire. All three stallions sired famous racehorses. Flying Childers, a chestnut foaled in 1715 by Darley Arabian, became the fastest horse ever to race at Newmarket. His speed and that of his siblings was unlike anything the English had ever seen, and thus was inaugurated a new epoch in the history of the sport and in the history of breeding. In the generations that immediately followed, the offspring of the three Arabian horses dominated as racers and in stud. Every horse registered in the stud books of all countries today traces in direct male line to one of the three stallions.

Crossing their progeny with English stock produced in time a leggy animal with a lean head, broad, flat forehead, full eyes, and small, pricked ears. It stood fifteen to sixteen hands high and weighed between 1,000 and 1,400 pounds. Colored bay, or brown, or chestnut, with occasional grays, roans, or blacks, the Thoroughbred was a spirited, high-strung animal whose conformation made him ideal for racing.

Shortly after the American Revolution, English stallions and mares began to be imported to this country quite regularly. One of the most famous imports of the 18th century was Messenger, who was brought to the colonies in 1788 at the age of 7½ years. A descendant of Flying Childers, he had already achieved remarkable renown as a racer at Newmarket in England. He was a gray standing fifteen hands three inches high. He stood at stud for more than twenty years in Philadelphia and in New York City, and his progeny became famous on both the running and trotting tracks. (He is considered the "fountainhead" of American trotters. His grandson Abdallah was mated to a trotting mare and sired Rysdyk's Hambletonian. Foaled in 1849, this potent sire produced 1,333 foals of record. One hundred fifty of his "better sons" sired 1,487 trotters and 220 pacers while eighty select daughters foaled 110 trotters and seven pacers, all fast enough to appear in record books. Thus, from the offspring of one sire, the American standardbred horse registry was established. These horses are known as Hambletonians.) It was also from Messenger that grays descended in this country. When he died in 1808, he was so widely beloved that he was given a military burial with soldiers firing volley after volley over his grave.

The Virginians who emigrated to Kentucky brought with them their well-established appreciation of fine horses and knowledge of breeding and bloodstock. During the Civil War, many eastern farmers relocated their Thoroughbred nurseries in Kentucky to escape the ravages of the war. They stayed in Kentucky after the war, enhancing the state's reputation as a natural place to raise good horses.

Robert Aitcheson Alexander, a native Kentuckian, is worthy of special note for the role he played in the breeding of Thoroughbreds in this country. He established Woodburn Farm in Kentucky. There, he applied both fortune and intelligence to the business of breeding. He acquired the stallion Lexington, who was to prove incomparable as a sire of champion horses. He began to record in great detail the names of the sires and dams he bred so that he might arrange breedings selectively. His procedures and standards for breeding were widely emulated and deeply influential.

The advertisements in today's trade magazines like *The Thoroughbred Record* and *The Blood-Horse* are spectacular, full-color photos of magnificent horses flying over finish lines throughout the world, whether it be Churchill Downs, or Epsom Downs, or the Irish

Sweepstakes. There are portraits of stallions standing at ease, their muscles gleaming. Their legs are slightly astraddle to show their anatomy to full advantage. They look as if they were royalty posing for a court painter, showing off for posterity their jambs and the power and sleekness of their muscles. They proclaim the dominance of their bloodline and help to promote and perpetuate the mystique of Kentucky-bred horses. Bold copy announces their big wins, their total earnings, their most gifted progeny, and, in some instances, their stud fees:

Northern Baby. Heir to the Northern Dancer dynasty. Group I stakes winner from a superb family. Won or placed in 12 of his 17 starts; brilliant at the classic 1¼-mile distance. Winner of England's prestigious Champion Stakes, the Prix Dollar and the Prix de la Cote Normande in France.

Seattle Slew. His 1985 Book including 9 champions, 28 graded group stakes winners, 18 graded group stakes producers, 39 stakes winners, 22 stakes producers.

Silver Hawk. Roberto—Gris Vitesse, by Amerigo. Silver Hawk won or placed in seven of his eight starts including the Epsom Derby (Gr. I), the Irish Sweeps Derby (Gr. I), the Royal Lodge Stakes (Gr. II) and the Ladbrokes Craven Stakes (Gr. III). Silver Hawk is out of French Group I winner Gris Vitesse, and his next two dams are also Group winners which went on to produce Group winners. The first foals by Silver Hawk are yearlings in 1985 and they're most exciting individuals.

Native Charger. Sire of 35 stakes winners! Native Charger has sired 35 stakes winners and 28 of his runners have placed in stakes. He ranks among the top 65 leading active sires lifetime, and also ranks among the top 65 broodmare sires for 1985. 1985 fee: $20,000.

In the same magazines regularly appear directories of Kentucky stud farms that list the stallions and a brief history of the farm's past breeding successes:

Buck Pond Farm Inc. Established by Colonel Thomas Marshall in 1783, Buck Pond occupies 300 rolling acres in a most fertile region of Woodford County. Champions Spectacular Bid, Lord Avie were born on the farm, as were Gay Mecene and Dactylographer. 50 mares.

Calumet Farm. Bred Triple Crown winners Whirlaway and Citation, also Armed, Bewitch, Alydar.

Claiborne Farm. Stallions: Ack Ack, Believe It, Coastal, Cox's Ridge, Damascus, Danzig, Drone, Honest Pleasure, Key to Content, Majestic Light, Mr. Prospector, Nijinsky II, Private Account, Riva Ridge, Secretariat, Sir Ivor, Spectacular Bid, Tom Rolfe, Avatar, Buckfinder, Hawaii, It's True, Le Fabuleux, Navajo, Topsider, Quadratic, Forli.

Golden Chance Farm. Breeders of world's leading money-winner John Henry.

Plum Lane Farm. In operation for Thoroughbreds since 1900. Stood Man o' War for first two years at stud, 90 mares.

Stone Farm. Began in May 1970 with two mares and 100 leased acres; now covers 2,500 acres and boards 450 horses, including 9 stallions and 200 mares.

The ads make it look easy: Choose your stallion, pay the stud fee, make an appointment for your mare, and simply decide which of the grand stakes races you want to enter. The breeding farms board horses, train them, breed them, and they sell yearlings. According to a survey conducted in 1984 by the Kentucky Thoroughbred Association, Inc., the median-sized horse farm is 160 acres and produces and registers six Kentucky-bred foals. The largest farms number thousands of acres, the smallest, under ten acres. Big breeder or small, it is selling stallion seasons and yearlings that provides the potential for real profit.

Thoroughbred champions are so highly valued at stud that often the ownership of a horse is divided into shares, or syndicated, both to reduce the cost per owner and to spread the risk. The number of shares is usually limited to forty, the approximate number of mares a stud will service in a breeding season. The shares are usually not sold over the counter, but are restricted to members of the horse world, those who know and appreciate the value of the stud and will help to perpetuate the quality of its bloodline. Each share entitles the owner to breed one mare to the stallion each breeding season over the lifetime of the stallion. Some shares are sold on a live-foal

guarantee basis, meaning that the mare must drop a live foal for the contract to be valid. And some are sold without guarantee, which means that if the mare drops a stillborn animal, the owner must swallow hard and walk away with nothing to show for his investment.

Mares don't always go into foal the first time they breed. Each share entitles the owner to breed a mare to the stallion up to five times in a season. If the stallion "fires a blank," or there is other difficulty, the owner can return up to four more times during that season. The average number of covers necessary to impregnate the mare is 1.75.

Horses in the wild breed in the spring and foal the following spring to take advantage of the new grass and warmer weather. Man was reluctant to try to disturb that cycle because the cost of boarding yearlings was much lower in good weather when there was pasture than in winter when they had to be housed, fed, and cared for more intensely. In modern times, however, man discovered that the hormonal changes that signal the approach of breeding season in a mare are affected by the amount of daylight, hence, the length of the days. By placing fluorescent lights in a mare's stall early in the winter, and by increasing the amount of protein in a mare's diet, man has moved up the cycle. The mares are ready to begin breeding in early February. The season continues through June. Owners who hope to race their horses as two-year-olds are especially anxious to have early foals, because a foal is recorded as being one year old on the first day of January following the birthdate. A foal born late in the year must race against two-year-olds who are likely to be more physically mature and stronger.

Each spring, convoys of horse vans journey to Kentucky carrying rich-blooded princesses and queens to be mated. They come from all over the world, by plane and van, swelling the horse population of the average breeding farm by as much as 50 percent.

The early days of itinerant breeders leading their stallions from town to town are gone forever. The stallions are so valuable that the risk of injury is a deterrent to travel. It is much more expedient to have the mares come to them. It is also true that a stallion's influence in establishing pedigree is far more widespread than that of a mare. Stallion owners schedule breeding appointments like doctors' offices. If the demand is such, the farm will breed its stallions twice a day, usually early in the morning and late afternoon. There is nothing magic about the schedule. It is arranged at the convenience of the farm, not the horses. The farm office books the appointments, bills

the clients, and keeps track of who is breeding to whom. In selecting the proper mate for his horse, the owner may consult an independent bloodstock agent to study the parentage and help him determine the best bloodlines. The computer has greatly enhanced the breeder's ability to improve his stock by providing him immediate access to information about pedigree. The decisions about breeding must be carefully calculated and may require a long timeline before the success or lack of it becomes evident. Olin Gentry began working on the bloodline that produced Roberto, the winner of the 1972 Epsom Derby, as far back as the 1920s. As a general rule, horsemen pay closest attention to the top line in a pedigree, the tail-male, through male issue.

At the appointed hour, the owner of the mare arrives with his mare. She is led into the breeding shed. A further example of specialized evolution—a tobacco shed or a barn once served the same purpose—the breeding shed is a clean, sparsely furnished barn built exclusively for breeding. It has large, padded rooms free of protrusions like nails and spikes and pegs—anything that might injure a horse or a man trying to get out of the way of a frightened horse. Aluminum buckets are neatly stacked in a small washroom. Each bucket has the name of one of the farm's breeding stallions stenciled on its side. The buckets are never interchanged as a further safeguard

against spreading infection or disease. The mare is taken into one
of the open-ended chambers and, if she appears nervous, petted and
calmed. In the meantime, from a distant pasture, a stallion has been
led into an adjoining room. He whinnies and snorts as he catches the
scent that a mare emits during oestrus.

What is about to transpire is only the prologue to the play. This
early-arriving stallion is not a Thoroughbred, but a standardbred
whose role in this instance is to tease the mare. He is referred to as
the teaser, and he is an essential actor in the commercial breeding
cycle. If the mare is in heat, she will probably be quietly submissive.

If the mare is not really in heat, however, she will reject the passionate advances of her suitor. If she cannot run away, she will show her disdain by trying to kick the stallion. The breeder of a multimillion-dollar stallion would rather first risk injury to a two-bit teaser.

The mare is backed up against the wall of the adjoining room where the teaser is. A panel in the wall is opened and the teaser, with a cry of anguish, plunges his nose into the mare's rear, snorting and grunting, trying to push his way through the restraining wall. The mare stands quietly, indicating she is ready to accept the stallion. The

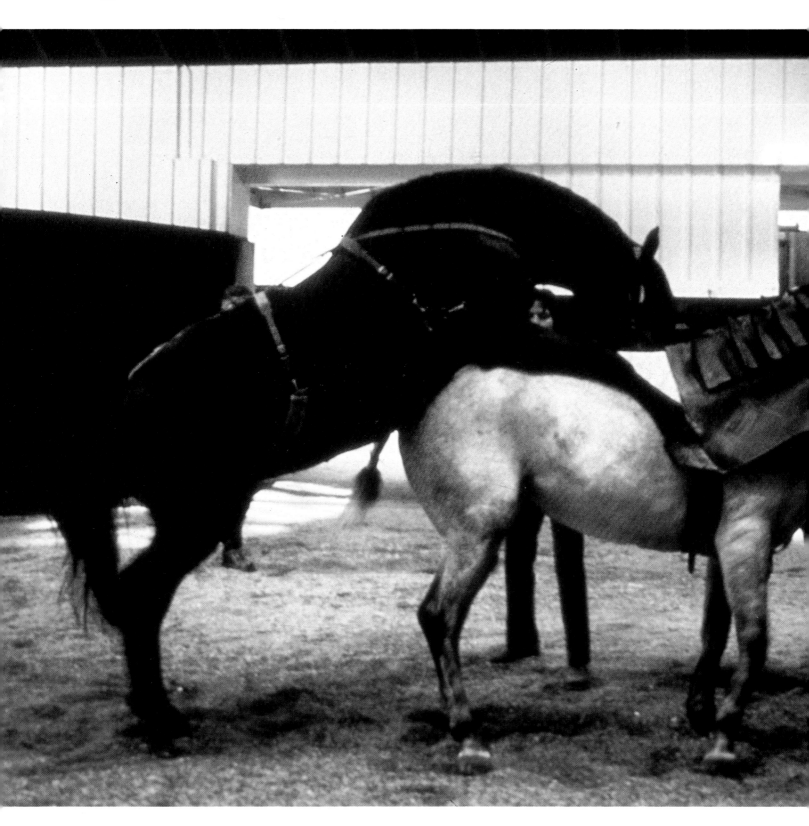

door is quickly slammed shut on the teaser, locking him into the darkness of his room, where he is left still trembling, no doubt pondering his strange fate, until the next breeding appointment.

The mare is led to another room in the shed, where she is hobbled and prepared for the real thing. A stable hand takes a twitch, a sturdy oak stick with a rawhide loop at the end, and places the thong over the mare's muzzle. He twists the loop several times until he has a secure hold on the mare's nose. The hobble and the twitch are normal precautions to try to prevent the mare if she becomes skittish from breaking free and injuring herself or the stallion. It is a relatively routine occurrence for a mare to jerk her head free with such power that she sends the twitch flying, and the stable hand with it. It is not unusual for stable hands to have to chase after a mare who has broken free and bolted from the shed. Her tail is wrapped with bandage so that a stray hair won't injure the stallion's penis, an injury that could cost the farm millions of dollars in stud fees. The vulva lips at the entrance to the mare's vagina are washed and the animal is ready to be bred.

Meanwhile, his lordship the stallion has been sent for. He arrives with seeming nonchalance, though he will most likely have started his erection halfway to the barn. When he arrives at the shed, his penis is washed with water from his own bucket. He is not allowed to rush the mare, but is led carefully to her. One of the crew of men who supervise the breeding has an apparatus that resembles a rolling pin wrapped with foam rubber. As the stallion rises on its hind legs and dances toward the mare, he places the rolling pin under the stallion's stomach to buffer the shock of the two enormous bodies making contact. Every precaution is taken to bring about as quick and successful a consummation as possible. The animals are carefully watched for any wrong moves that could signal trouble. If the stallion thrusts wildly, the crew will take his penis and guide it. The brief moment of ardor has little romance about it: Twelve hundred pounds of prima-donna sinew and muscle stands on its hind legs, grunting and snorting as if he were a primeval beast instead of a million-dollar business. When the stallion is finished and descends, he is washed again and led quickly away, not having seen any more of the mare than her rear end.

The stallion may breed again that same day, or breed once a day, or breed only a few times a week. It depends on the animal.

A stallion is considered mature at three years and an adult at five. Adult stallions may handle a book of up to fifty mares a season. While fecundity with Thoroughbreds can last beyond the age of twenty, as a rule, their load is reduced as they become older. The animals are carefully monitored, their feeding habits watched closely, and blood tests administered if necessary to make sure the stallion is not wearing out.

Twenty-eight days after breeding, the mare is usually examined with ultrasound to see if she is pregnant. If she is not, she will come back into heat two to three weeks after the previous heat. The mare may show signs of being pregnant when in fact she is not. To ensure conception, a stallion can be bred to a mare every second or third day of the heat, but it is more common today to examine her uterus with ultrasound. It is not unusual during breeding season for a visitor to a horse farm to see a veterinarian standing in a barn with his arm immersed up to his shoulder in the rectum of a mare, holding the monitor to an ultrasound imaging machine, peering at a small television screen at his feet. (An X-ray strong enough to pass through the horse's abdomen would cause radiation burns.) It is likely only one of dozens of such examinations he will conduct before his day finishes. A picture of the inside of the mare's uterus is transmitted to

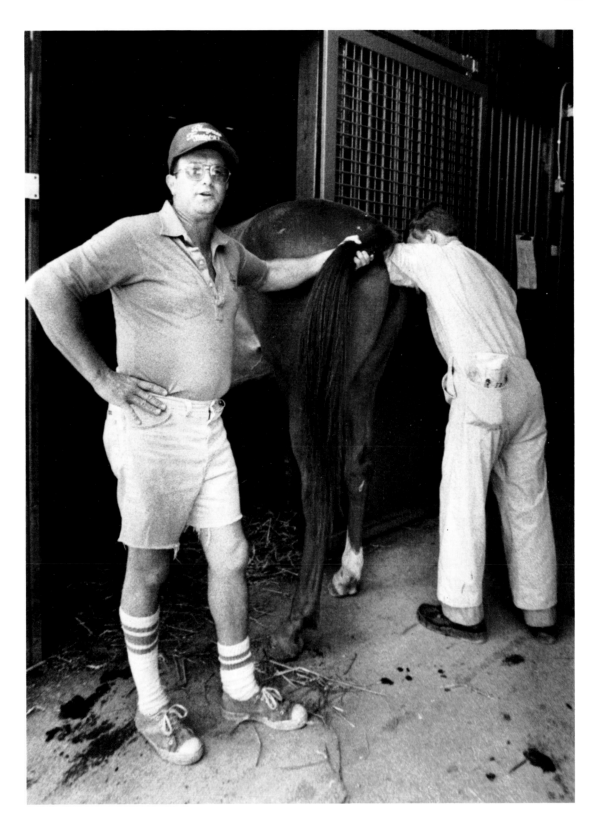

the screen. If there is a foetus in the ovary, it will be possible to see its heart beating. Usually, the vet can tell by gently feeling the ovary whether there is a foetus. At this juncture, it will be the size of a grape. A mare usually produces one foal per mating, but on occasion, the vet will discover two grapes in the ovary, twins. He will immediately abort one by simply squeezing it. Both twins seldom survive a pregnancy. Even if they did, it is likely both would be smaller than normal and less attractive in the auction ring.

Gestation lasts eleven months. While the mare carries the foal, she can do most anything—as is to be expected from her origin as a wild animal. There are various drugs that can be administered to help the mare hold the pregnancy if there is some history of miscarriage.

Approaching the final stage of her pregnancy, she is put into her stall and watched day and night. She will indicate the imminent moment by becoming very restless, often lying down, then standing right back up, circling her stall, pawing the ground. Labor is usually short, seldom more than an hour, and the actual birth is a matter of minutes. The mare expels the foal front feet and head first and usually rises to her feet immediately after birth, a throwback, again, to her instinct for safety and survival in the wilderness. Foaling seems to be regarded by most mares as a private matter, and some mares may actually try to retain the foal if there are spectators present. When her baby is born, the mare is likely to become extremely protective and may radically alter her personality.

Within a short time—ten to fifteen minutes—the foal will try to get to its feet. After a few wobbly ventures, the foal will finally succeed in standing and will begin to nurse. The short period between birth and movement is another result of the horse's evolution as a wild animal dependent on speed and ability to keep up with the herd. The foal can begin to travel in a matter of hours. This is due, in part, to its long legs, which are already nearly as long as they will be when the horse is fully grown. In fact, the cannon bone, which connects the knee to the fetlock or ankle, is as long as it will ever be.

The life of a foal is a pampered one. He nurses for six months before he is weaned, although long before that he will have begun imitating his mother nibbling grass. The colt's first moments of real anguish occur when he is stabled out of sight of his mother. There is considerable heart-wrenching whinnying for about a week, but by the end of a month or so, the colt will have lost interest in his mother's

milk and the mare's milk will have dried up. In the meantime, the foal's principal occupation will be eating, as many as four meals a day. Most trainers try to accustom the foal to handling very early. Halters may be put on within a few hours after birth. They will get the colt used to being led for short distances. The object is gradually to get the animal used to people and halters, and to having his feet examined. Raising a good horse means treating him gently but firmly. A mistreated animal or a spoiled brat will be much harder to train.

A Thoroughbred foal must be registered with The Jockey Club no later than the last day of its two-year-old year. The foal's sex and

color, the name of its sire and dam, the date and location of foaling, a complete written description of its markings, as well as the names and addresses of the breeder and foal owner, must be included in the application for registration. Photographs of the horse showing front, both sides, and back must also be presented. As a further means of identification, the horse must be bloodtyped. Owners must also tattoo the inside of the horse's lip with a number.

If the foal is to be sold as a yearling, it will remain unnamed. But if the owner wishes to register a name for the horse, he must adhere to strict guidelines. For example, the following classes of names are not eligible for use:

– Names with more than eighteen letters, including spaces and punctuation marks.

– Initials such as C.O.D., F.O.B., etc.

– Names of living persons unless written permission to use their name is on file with The Jockey Club.

– Names of famous or notorious people.

– Names of racetracks.

– Names that are suggestive or have a vulgar or obscene meaning.

– Names that are currently active in the stud or on the turf and names similar in spelling or pronunciation to these names.

– Names that have been used during the preceding ten years either in stud or on the turf, except that names of geldings reported dead may be used five years after death.

These and the other rules notwithstanding, the naming of racehorses has always afforded ample opportunity for creativity, and the names of horses over the centuries have formed a rich genre in the literature of sport.

As the foals grow and become yearlings, economic considerations reassert themselves. The owner must decide their fates. If he is to sell them, he must begin preparing them for the auctions. In any case, he must cull his herd and make some hard choices. Up to this point, pedigree has been the force that shaped his decisions about breeding. And it is pedigree he will try to sell in the auction ring. But the animal must look the part, even if it never plays the part on the racetrack. Good conformation means a lot in the preliminary assessment of a horse's potential and in how much money it will command in the auction ring.

Some horses look and move like athletes, just as some humans do. Overall proportion and grace of movement are key. A head that is too small usually indicates the animal will lack size when it is mature. Large heads on yearlings are not unnatural and generally indicate growth to come, though a too-large, massive head is undesirable. Naturally, the shape of the head does not necessarily affect how the animal will run, but in the early stages, it counts in the auction ring, particularly if the horse is to be trained for show. We have already said that the ears should be perky, alert, not loppy or mulish-looking. The horse's eye should be large, without being "pop" or bovine. Buyers like the promise of a bright, kindly eye and they avoid horses with pig eyes. Large nostrils are seen as an indication of good breathing capacity. The horse's mouth must align correctly. Monkey and parrot mouths—underbites and overbites—are undesirable, as they may lead to trouble in properly chewing and masticating the food, and to problems with digestion.

A horse's teeth are important for further ensuring that dental problems will not complicate the task of digesting food, a task that seems already complex and fraught with problems for the horse. It's

worth a minute of digression to point out that a horse's teeth are not an authentic way to determine its age, as is popularly believed. A horse's age can be judged fairly accurately by the condition of its front teeth or incisors until it is about six years old. The mouth undergoes different structural changes while the horse is a youngster. Teeth come and go until the sixth year. By then, the permanent teeth are in place and there will be no further structural change. Guessing the horse's age after that will depend mainly on correctly gauging the amount of wear and tear on the teeth and gums. As the young horse's new teeth come into place, they have an indentation in the top center of each tooth that captures food particles that decay and blacken the space, often staining the teeth down through the enamel to the dentine. The sides of the hollow on each tooth are gradually worn down and the marks gone by the time a horse is nine. After nine, the teeth begin to change their shape at the top from a broad lateral shape to a triangular one. By the time the horse is very old, the depth of the teeth from front to rear exceeds the lateral width. Unscrupulous horse dealers in days of old used to try to disguise horses older than nine by marking their teeth with acid. A knowledgeable horseman could uncover the deception by noting the shape of the tops of the teeth.

The preferred shape of the Thoroughbred's neck is long and slender. The withers behind the crest of the neck is the point from which a horse's height is measured. Low, thick withers cramp a horse's motion and prevent a long stride with the front legs. A short, straight back with ''well-sprung'' ribs is strongly preferred to a ''roach'' back (convex), or a swayback. A swayback horse looks as if he is about to collapse in the middle. The horse's chest should be deep and broad. Too narrow a chest makes the legs appear to come out of ''one hole.'' Too wide a chest may result in the legs being set too far apart. A deep chest suggests ample capacity for strong lungs and heart.

When horses walk, their stride should be free and fluid, a smooth meshing of bone and muscle. Some horses walk funny—like penguins wearing flippers. Others are pigeon-toed. Some are knock-kneed, as if their mothers were bred by bulls and dropped foals that should have grown into veal chops instead. The horse's shoulder blade is attached to the body solely by muscles, unlike the human shoulder, which has a skeletal attachment. A long, sloping shoulder

will allow a longer, more powerful stride and higher action of the front legs. And, by reason of the greater angle it forms with the horse's forelimb, it also offers greater shock-absorbing ability. The forearm should be long, again to allow for a long stride. The knee hinges the forearm to the cannon and should be wide and thick and able to take a lot of wear and tear.

Horsemen look carefully at the placement of the knee. If the knee is set too far forward in proportion to the rest of the leg, it is considered "knee-sprung": too far back, calf-kneed. A knock-kneed horse has its knees set inward, while a bow-kneed horse has its knees set outward. The cannon connects the knee to the fetlock or horse's ankle. The ankle is another joint that must absorb a lot of concussion, especially when the weight of the horse is thrown on the pasterns, the section of the horse's foot beneath the fetlock. It is important that the pasterns not be too long, nor too short, and that they be set at just the right angle to the leg, approximately 45 degrees. When the horse gallops and throws almost its entire weight on one leg momentarily, the pastern is bent to almost 90 degrees. Too long or too straight a pastern will reduce its ability to play a role in the horse's shock-absorbing system. Good pasterns are said to add spring and snap to a horse's stride. It is not uncommon for horses to bruise their pasterns on the track as they run, the more so if the angle of the pastern is awry.

The horse's hoof is likewise constructed to cushion as well as drive the horse forward. The frog, a horny, triangular pad, is the main cushion. The horn acts somewhat like a toenail and grows at the rate of about one-half inch a month. As the new horn wears down, the old horn of the frog and sole wears and flakes off.

The hindquarters of the horse are its main propelling mechanism. The hock joints carry a tremendous amount of the workload. The direction of the set of the hock joints has considerable effect on a horse's performance as well as its appearance. Too great an angle in or out can cause added stress on the knees and lead to lameness or breakdown. Even the tail is considered important in judging a horse's appearance. Buyers like to see a tail well set—it suggests a strong tailbone.

"Pretty is as pretty does on the track." And: "The perfect ones don't run." These two cliches are cliches with real meaning. Assault, who won the Kentucky Derby in 1946, had a clubbed front right hoof as the result of an accident suffered when he was a colt. He stepped on a surveyor's stake, which pierced the frog of his hoof. The injury healed, but his hoof was permanently deformed, and he walked with a limp the rest of his life. He was also a small horse, weighing less than 1,000 pounds and standing barely fifteen hands high. Canonero II, who won the Derby in 1971, was another less-than-perfect specimen of horseflesh. He had a crooked leg.

While horsemen disagree on lots of things about a horse's conformation, they generally agree that conformation tells nothing about a horse's courage. The great racers have one thing in common besides speed, and that is courage. Mel Heimer, in his book *Inside Racing* (Van Nostrand, 1967), tells the story of one of the most courageous of horses, Dark Secret, trying at the age of five to win his second successive Jockey Club Gold Cup on a muddy track. After two miles of a "bitter ding-dong duel" with another horse, Dark Secret came to the homestretch with a slight lead, but misstepped and almost fell. As the second-place horse approached, Dark Secret seemed to gather himself and get back into stride, driving for the wire and winning by a nose. Just beyond the wire, he almost fell again. The jockey pulled him up and jumped from the saddle. Dark Secret

stood there with one of his legs dangling beneath him, broken
beyond repair. He had won, but the price of victory was
his destruction.

The only true test for courage is to put the horse in a race and see
how he responds. There is more, however, to racing than just putting

a horse in a race. He must learn how to run. If he is to become a racer, once he leaves the auction ring, his new career commences in earnest, driven again mostly by the economics of breeding, which are compelling.

A stud fee can range from peanuts to six figures. If we assume a moderate fee, by way of example, of $7,500 and multiply it by forty or fifty mares, the total fees range from $300,000 to $375,000 earned by a single stallion in a single season. A large operation with nine or ten stallions can make millions just on stud fees. Then there are the yearlings. In 1984, 7,014 Thoroughbred yearlings were sold at Kentucky auctions for a whopping grand total of $481,832,000. The overall average sale price for Thoroughbred yearlings was $77,000, compared to an average price of $41,396 for all yearlings sold at auction in North America in the same year. The median price for a horse at a Kentucky auction was $17,000, compared to a national figure of $6,500.

The other side of the picture is a lot less compelling. First, the national figure of $6,500 was the lowest since 1978, and only $500 higher than the 1978 figure. The downward drift caused by the proliferation of foals is one of the major worries in the industry. There has been a dramatic increase in the number of foals throughout the continent over the past twenty years or so. In 1962, fewer than 15,000 foals were registered as Thoroughbreds, whereas, in 1982, more than 41,000 were, an increase of more than 160 percent. The rate of increase per annum has doubled in recent years from an annual figure of no higher than 5 percent to one of 10.2 percent in 1981–82. Kentucky has led all other states in Thoroughbred foal production since 1972—producing 16 percent of the 321,622 Thoroughbreds foaled in the decade from 1973 to 1982, more than twice as many as the next closest state, California, with 12.6 percent. Kentucky produced 9,000 Thoroughbred foals in 1984. Between 1980 and 1982, its foal production increased 27 percent, reflecting what is happening nationally.

Second, it costs about $15,000 to $18,000 to bring a Kentucky-bred yearling to auction, not including the stud fee. The rule of thumb is that the owner of the yearling has to make two to three times the stud fee to break even. Assuming a moderate stud fee, he can't regain his investment unless he can sell the yearling above the median price.

Third, there is the unmentionable problem of what to do with horses that don't make the grade as racers or breeders. The average Thoroughbred horse lives about twenty years, some up to thirty and thirty-five . A horse that is nonproductive as an investment represents a consumer in the strictest sense, a sinkhole for money for feed and care. Unless there is a place for such an animal in a different role—as a riding horse or a nurse mare—or some way the animal can perform a useful function, it may be expedient for the owner to dispose of the animal. Such animals disappear quietly. Such a seemingly inglorious ending does not easily fit the romantic notions of horse racing, and thus is not widely publicized. But, for some owners who lack the resources, either in money or space, to take on large numbers of boarders in perpetuity, it is an economic reality, not unlike disposing of cars that have begun to cost more than they are worth.

Unlike junked cars, however, horses continue to serve man even in death. Horsemeat is still popular in Europe, particularly among the French, whose butcher shops carry it fresh. Horsemeat makes up the meat content of many pet foods. The bones and cartilage are used to make glue. Shoes and belts are made from horsehide—the original cordovan leather used by the Moors in Cordoba, Spain, came from horsehide. Horsehairs are used in upholstery, mattresses, lining for coats and suits, and, in some cases, for violin bows.

The significance of all the figures is twofold. One, the number of foals in this country is proliferating, with a subsequent decline in their value—except at the tip-top, where the demand is pushing value the other way, toward higher prices. Only 1 percent of the Thoroughbred yearlings sold at auction in North America in 1984 sold for more than $500,000.

Two, in spite of this ominous trend, Kentucky-bred and -sired yearlings continue to look better to horsemen. Throughout the decade cited above, Kentucky has remained North America's leading producer of stakes winners, with 28 percent. Of the 111 Kentucky Derbys that have been run, eighty-four have been won by horses foaled in the Commonwealth. The 28 percent figure is more than twice that of second-place Florida, with 12.6 percent, and, with the exception of one year, 1981, has been twice the number of the second-place state every year since 1973. The conclusion is obvious: Kentucky horses not only look better, they are better.

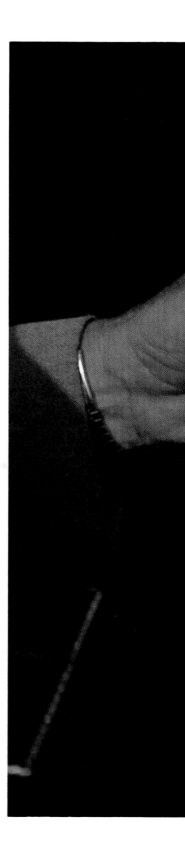

There is a story about a horse that won the Kentucky Derby. In the hours immediately following the race, after the horse had been returned to its barn in the backstretch at Churchill Downs, one of the animal's grooms sat drinking a can of beer, relaxing from the emotional high of the afternoon. He suddenly heard sounds that suggested the owner and some friends were approaching. He knew the owner was a teetotaler and would be unhappy to see him drinking, but he had no time to hide the beer. In desperation, he flung the can into the champion's stall. Alas, not the owner but one of his friends spied the can half-buried in the straw and, not wishing to

Training the Four-Legged Athlete

betray his ignorance, took the groom aside and asked why it was there. The groom explained it was customary to give the champ a can of beer with his morning feed on the day of a race, and he had simply forgotten to pick up the empty. Shortly after, other trainers began feeding beer to their charges before races.

That apocryphal story has a moral: Training racehorses is a science and an art, as susceptible to fancy as it is dependent on fact. Ask ten trainers how to train a horse and you will likely get ten different answers. The trainer's job, pure and simple, is to get racehorses in shape to win races. Not surprisingly, the good trainers are those who have a keen knowledge of the animal, experience, the wisdom of Solomon, and not a little bit of luck. They search constantly for that "edge," that special, secret technique that gives their horse the advantage. Even if he should find a magic potion, he still cannot turn a nag into Man o' War. But he can make an important difference in how the horse performs.

The role of the trainer has evolved quite dramatically through history. At the beginning of the 19th century, most trainers were low-paid servants who served as both groom and trainer. By the end of the same century, it was quite an ordinary occurrence to see the

English trainer "'tall-hatted, frock-coated, kid-gloved and patent-leather-booted' dwelling in a 'handsome and comfortable residence . . . with fine gardens, trim lawns for croquet and lawn-tennis, billiard rooms, and cellars containing choice vintages.'" (From *Racing and Steeplechasing* (1886) by the Earl of Suffolk; quoted in *The Turf: A Social and Economic History of Horse-Racing*, 1976, by Wray Vamplew.)

Today, the trainer's name is quite often listed next to the jockey's name in reporting the winning horses of a major race. The trainer may have anywhere from a handful of horses to a string of a hundred or so in his care. He may believe in "a lot of long, slow works" or in making his horses tough through lots of tough workouts. Whichever the case, they are as varied and inscrutable a group as the horses they supervise.

The decision to train a yearling as a racehorse is both an end and a beginning for the youngster. If he is to be raced, he must learn how to run.

The first step for the buyer of a yearling at the Keeneland auction, or elsewhere, is to take him to a good veterinarian and have him X-rayed head to toe. The vet will check the knees, the ankles, the hocks. He'll endoscope him—check his throat and look for wind problems. The sound that a horseman dreads most is a whistling or roaring noise that indicates the airway through the larynx is reduced and the horse may have difficulty inhaling sufficient air when it is running.

While no one would risk the disgrace and the legal ramifications

that might ensue from knowingly selling a faulty animal at Keeneland, it is also true, in the words of one trainer, "nobody goes to the sale and lets his bare butt hang out." Examining the horse for undetected defects is a prerequisite to training him. The animal will get a thorough critique of its conformation and the vet will recommend at this juncture whether or not to race him as a two-year-old or to wait another year. Some trainers never race two-year-olds, fearing that the pounding of the racetracks will break down the horse's legs. Others whisk the animals off to warm weather places like Florida and begin intensive preparation for racing right away.

In either case, it takes six weeks, ideally, to break the yearlings, and another two to three months, at least, to train them for racing. That means not only getting them into running shape, but teaching them how to run in a race. Prior to the sales, the yearlings have only been taught to be handled, to stand, to be led and groomed. They are not in racing shape. Sixty days will suffice if the owner is in a hurry, but trainers prefer the longer period. In that time, they "put a mouth on him," or get him used to a bridle; they accustom him to a saddle; and they break him or ride him.

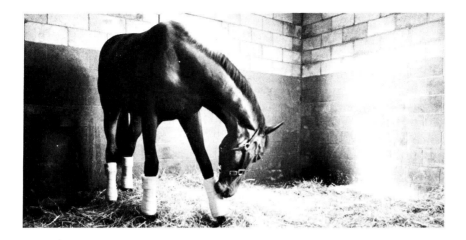

In the lower jaw of a horse's mouth, between the incisors and the molar teeth in mares, and the canines and the molars in stallions, are gum surfaces known as bars, which are covered with mucous membranes and are sensitive to pressure. It is upon these bars that the pressure of the bit is brought to bear. (When this mucous membrane becomes toughened and calloused, the sensitivity of the horse's mouth is deadened and the animal is said to be hardmouthed.) The horse's tongue also helps support and receive pressure from the bit and receive signals from the reins. When the trainer first puts a bridle on his young athlete, he does not necessarily hook it up right away. He may let it hang loose for two or three days, letting the horse get used to having it in his mouth.

When it comes time to ride the horse, the trainer will strap the saddle on and nothing else at first, letting him adjust. Then, he'll put a rider on his back in the stall, turn him around, do left and right turns, figure 8s, a little each day, nothing too traumatic. He doesn't want to "spook" or scare the horse and disrupt his training cycle. The Thoroughbred's ancestry as a wild animal whose safety lay in never-ending vigilance and fleetness has left as its legacy a naturally nervous and high-strung animal, easily startled and suspicious. The bite of a fly, a loud noise, a sudden movement, a strange sight—any and all have been known to startle the animal whose first instinct is to flee to evade danger. Horses often show panic as a reaction. For example, horses will run back into a burning barn. While horses will often strike out with their heels, it is more a defensive action than an attack, although there are instances where a horse brutalized by its

owner has been known to attack him. This natural nervousness is the root of most troubles that Thoroughbreds get into.

Although a random poll of Kentucky horsemen, or, for that matter, any horsemen the world over, will elicit a wide range of opinions about the animal's native intelligence, the fact is that horses seem to have little reasoning ability. It is true that some horses have been known to learn how to open the latch of their stalls or the lid of a container of feed, and that some seem to anticipate their rider's commands. But, the virtues of Kentucky bluegrass notwithstanding, horses rank rather low in the hierarchy of animal intelligence—much lower, for instance, than pigs. They compensate to some extent by having finely honed instincts and by being outstanding creatures of habit. They hear well and have a good sense of smell. They seem able to sense water and fire and impending danger. They have an uncanny sense of direction. And they can sense a rider's uncertainty, his nervousness, or his fear, which explains why horses are often so unsettled before a race—they have picked up the nervousness of the men around them. Their visual and auditory memories are such that they may remember the unpleasantness of a bad thunderstorm or a cruel trainer for many years afterward. Often, a trainer will vary his tone of voice and his words in such a way that the horse can associate them with desired movements. Horses remember well often-repeated signals, particularly signals "of the cupboard variety." The knowledge that some delectable tidbit—a carrot or an apple or a cube of sugar—awaits the right response is a powerful motivator.

By the end of four weeks or so, the trainer will have the yearling outside its stall. At first, he may walk him up and down the hallway of the barn. Then it's out to the paddock to walk him, trot him, play with him. If the horse is not to race for another year, the trainer will ease up on him during the winter. He'll let him relax in the paddock, see the trees and woods, enjoy life as a youngster. Such low-key training is known as "hacking" the horses. If the owner—whom, we mustn't forget, is paying the trainer to school his horse, unless it is a situation where the trainer works for the owner as a salaried employee, which is often the case on the large training farms—wishes to minimize his expenses, he may have the trainer turn his horses out through the winter, stop intensive training until the spring.

Whatever schedule is dictated by the owner's desire, at some point the trainer begins "legging up" the horse, jogging him two

to four miles a day. The roadwork is designed to muscle him up, put "some bottom on him." The trainer wants to give him lungs without the concussion caused by the hard pounding of sprinting. Gradually, the trainer will pick up the pace and let the horse go faster and faster.

Theories of training have changed dramatically over the years. Once upon a time, trainers believed in the adage "The more work, the better." Horses were run vigorously for long stretches at a time. One of England's leading trainers between 1810 and 1830 was William Chifney, whose father, Samuel (1753–1807), was a great jockey and invented the chifney bridle with a special bit that is used commonly today. Described by a contemporary as the "severest trainer of his time," he forced his horse to "eight-mile sweats and frequent and vigorous gallops, breaking down many in the process." (From *British Flat Racing*, by Roger Mortimer, Richard Onslow, Peter Willett, 1978, cited in *The Turf*, by Alan Ross. Oxford University Press, Oxford, England. 1982.)

"The animals might be worked for three hours at a time, being galloped several times and given drinks of water in between, then worked again in the evening. They were sweated, purged and dieted on horsebread consisting of beans, wheat and rye, ground up and baked, and fed a day old, and they were heavily clothed with their bellies girt in a swaddling-clothes manner. By the 19th century, training methods had become reasonable; horses were still exercised

at four or five o'clock in the morning and were out for two hours
or more, but were galloped less severely, and their feeding and
clothing approximated to that of the present time. The tendency,
today, is to give horses light work, seldom keep them at exercise for
more than an hour and a half, and to vary the routine of exercise.''

(From *The Turf,* by John Hislop, 1948, cited in *The Turf,* by Alan Ross, Oxford University Press, Oxford, England, 1982.)

A typical modern-day workout ranges from a half-mile breeze to a two-mile gallop, depending on what the trainer is trying to accomplish. A horse galloping across a pasture with its tail flying behind it is not running in the same way a horse running down the homestretch at Churchill Downs is. There the animal is extending itself, bending every corpuscle to the task of locomotion at a speed that can average close to forty miles per hour over a distance of ¾ to 1¼ miles. The horse must learn how to run hard and straight, how to

run alongside the rail, and how to run neck and neck with other horses. Teaching a horse to gallop in a straight line and as close to the rail as he can go is complicated by the fact that the horse must be taught not to run always on the rail. Otherwise, he will cut straight for the rail in a race and risk fouling other horses by taking their ground. The animal must learn to run past the gap in the rail where horses enter and leave the track and not think it is time to exit. Mahout, a heavy favorite in the Lawrence Realization at Belmont Park in 1946, raced the first eighth mile toward the clubhouse turn and then, as he neared the gap in the rail, suddenly tried to turn in and head for home. Eddie Arcaro was the jockey, and the surprise maneuver cost him the race. The young horse must learn how to ride in response to the jockey.

The trainer goes to the gates with his aspiring racer, at first every four or five days to get him used to the contraption that plays such an integral part in a horse's chance for success in a race.

As the trainer assesses the progress of his pupil, he may adjust techniques and strategies. He may change the bridle, varying the

pressure on one side of the horse's mouth to make him more or less responsive to directions to that side. He may add blinkers. (Whirlaway, the famous Triple Crown winner of 1941, wore one blinker over his right eye, the left cup having been torn off so he could see the rail.) He may resort to such sophisticated techniques as gait analysis to determine the mechanical efficiency of the horse's running style, which, in turn, might affect training methods and how the horse is shod.

In 1880, Leland Stanford commissioned a photographer to help him win a wager by proving that a galloping horse put one leg down at a time and leaped, as opposed to the popular theory that the horse's gallop was a succession of leaps. The photographer laid out twenty cameras across a track at close intervals, with silk threads stretched across the track to trip the camera shutters. The galloping horse broke the threads and the photographs showed a four-beat movement, with the horse's legs resembling the spokes of a wheel. The legs made a revolution forward and backward. The hind legs push the animal forward onto its forelegs, which reach forward. Subsequent studies using high-speed cameras have shown that in a superior racehorse, no two feet touch down together longer than about .0081 second. The average racehorse covers about 2½ times its body length with each stride, a distance of about twenty-one to twenty-four feet, a stride being measured as the distance from the time one foot touches until the same foot touches again. A 1973 study of Secretariat in the Marlboro Cup at Belmont Park that year against Riva Ridge showed that both horses made the same number of strides. Each stride took .43 second. However, Secretariat's stride covered 23.8 feet, Riva Ridge's, 23.2 feet. The horse with the more efficient stride, in this instance, won. Secretariat's stride is one inch under twenty-five feet. Man o' War's stride measured twenty-five to twenty-eight feet.

Whatever the trainer does, in sum, he will do knowing that what works for one horse may not work for another. While scientists may chart the horse low on the ladder of animal intelligence, trainers consider a horse that learns the starting gate quickly to be pretty smart, whereas his stablemate who seems not to catch on as easily may hear a sobriquet or two implying some doubt about his native intelligence.

When a horse finishes its workout, it must be cooled off for

an hour or so, walked by a hot walker, a stable hand who walks the horse around the barn or paddock to cool it and keep it from getting stiff. They will likely bathe the horse, wash it, and cover it with a blanket to prevent it from cooling too rapidly. A horse's legs are so sensitive to overwork, or to blows or sprains, especially if the animal is young or has been worked on hard surfaces, that the

slightest blow to the legs seems to cause them to swell up. (Lameness may also be caused by bony growths, or soft-tissue swellings, or injury to the hooves.) The Thoroughbred's legs are the first object of a trainer's attention after any workout or race. The horse has bad circulation in its legs, so as a general theorem, everything a trainer does for the legs is to help circulation.

The pounding of the hooves causes the ankles to swell, so quite often after a workout, they may be packed in mud packs or poultices, or sleeves with liniment that wrap around the legs and draw out the heat. He may need a whirlpool, in which case he will stand, alternating his front and back legs in a portable whirlpool tub, looking like any other tired, million-dollar athlete. There are also newer forms of treatment. For instance, lame horses are being treated with acupuncture and laser technology to ease the pain of lameness. Researchers are studying ways to detect incipient lameness by using a track with embedded sensors that feed data on hoof pressure into a computer for analysis. With so much money at stake, a horse isn't necessarily doomed anymore by a broken leg. Broken legs are routinely rebuilt now with metal implants in operating rooms outfitted with electronic heart monitors and X-ray machines. The matter of disposing of a horse because it has broken its leg has always seemed extreme to those who do not understand the nature of the animal's legs, and how difficult, if not impossible, until relatively recent times, it has been for veterinarians and surgeons to treat broken legs successfully. To begin with, insurance companies make it easier to destroy a racehorse than to try to restore it. They require absolute proof that an animal is injured and unable to run again before they will pay off. And, putting aside the complex medical problem of correctly setting the bones of the leg so that it can once again provide the animal painless mobility, most surgical procedures on a horse's legs require some period of recuperation and relative immobility, a condition that in the past was impossible to achieve. A horse coming out of surgery and shock was often wild and uncontrollable. Now, there are devices—one is at the New Bolton Center in Pennsylvania —to hoist the horse from the operating table in a horse-shaped wet suit and float him in a swimming pool until he becomes calm. The veterinary school at Tufts University in Grafton, Massachusetts, is planning to build a sports-medicine center for horses that will include a sixty-foot swimming pool, Jacuzzi, and

treadmill designed for use by racehorses trying to make a comeback after surgery. (As another example of how veterinary medicine has become more sophisticated, there was the recent case of a prize show horse who suddenly started fainting and backing off his feed. Soon he was keeling over several times a day, banging into the walls of his stall. He was diagnosed ultimately as having contracted a virus that had damaged his heart. In what was a novel procedure, the horse was implanted with a pacemaker and was soon his same frisky self once again.)

Like any athlete, the racehorse is hungry after a workout, and like any athlete, the right diet is important to overall condition and success. Especially with horses. A horse's guts, more than one trainer has remarked, were put together by a committee. It has one small stomach—unlike its fellow grazer, the cow, for example, which has five. The cow's ample number of stomachs allows it to perform a highly valuable deworming service for horses. Horses, like all animals, have worms. They are susceptible to fifty different kinds. Cows and horses are often quartered together in the same pasture. Worms and their eggs are passed by the horse in its dung. The adult worms get up on the grass, where they are eaten by the cows without consequence because they die in the antechambers of the cow's digestive system. In pastures where only horses are quartered, the horses eat the worms and recycle them through their system, providing the worms additional opportunity to breed in their host. It is necessary, in such an instance, after deworming the horse, to let the pasture lie fallow for a month or more. The worms cannot survive more than thirty or forty days in sunlight, so they die and their life cycle is broken. We get some further idea of the value of this control factor when we consider that the horse passes about $\frac{1}{25}$ of its body weight in dung over a twenty-four--hour period—About forty-four pounds for a horse of 1,100 pounds—which in an infected horse may contain as many as ten million eggs.

The horse has a voluminous large colon, where the greatest part of its digestive activity occurs. Unlike in many other mammals, including humans, bacteria play a large part in digestion. The system is hypersensitive to spoiled feed, especially in warm weather. The most common digestive malady is colic, which occurs in many different forms and with varying degrees of gravity. One form with unusually violent effects is grass sickness, thought to be caused

by toxins produced by molds growing in the herbage the horse has eaten. The toxins damage the nerves in the intestines and the horse often dies.

Another form of colic is caused by the small intestine twisting into a knot, a development that is usually fatal unless surgically treated. Simple stoppage caused by a large accumulation of dry food, usually in the colon, is a painful but generally easily curable malady.

Short of eating rank grass or hay, a sudden, dramatic change in diet, improper exercise habits, eating too soon before or after exercising, improper watering, excitement—any of these can cause colic. While signs of colic may vary, the one constant symptom is refusal to take feed. The more violent colic will cause a horse to roll on its back and thrash with its legs. The usual treatment for the milder forms is to "oil them and walk them"—give the animal a laxative (salt, water, and liquid paraffin, for instance) and keep it walking about until the stoppage passes. If necessary, pain-killing drugs can be administered. Horses are constant feeders in the wild and, ironically, the bluegrass region has one of the highest colic rates in the country, particularly in the spring, when the horses cherish the fresh, tender grass and eat a lot of it. The farms like to cut the spring grass about every ten days. It keeps the grass young and tender and prevents it from becoming thick and stemmy. More to the point, it looks nicer when cut. Cutting, however, prevents the horse from getting the benefit of natural fiber that the longer grass would provide as it becomes lignified or more stemmy and fibrous. Many trainers regularly give their horses bran mash to supplement their feed. That is the best preventive medicine, that and making any dietary changes, or any change in the environment or routine, very gradual.

Otherwise, horses will eat almost anything from beer to sardines. Their main fare consists of oats, barley, wheat, cracked corn, and, often mixed in with part of one thing or another, a dessert of sweet molasses, and plenty of powdered and liquid vitamins, and red mineral salt. They will usually eat three meals a day, beginning with a quart of oats in the morning and another quart at brunch, along with a flake of sweet alfalfa hay. The big meal is dinner in the afternoon. Altogether, he'll munch through ten to twelve quarts of feed plus hay on a normal day. The oats may be crimped (mechanically "chewed"), the barley steamrolled, and hot water added to make a mash and ease digestion. During their racing days, they may

receive additional pellets of high protein and additional vitamins.
About 16 percent of a yearling's feed will be dedicated to protein.
And, of course, there is always fresh hay for roughage and fiber for
them to nibble on in their stalls. On racing days, a trainer will give his
horse a light meal—perhaps plain oats—in the morning and save the

main meal until evening. Periodic blood tests help the trainer monitor the horse's condition. Too much exercise, or too little, may cause the horse to back off his feed.

It costs about $40 a day to feed and groom a Thoroughbred in the style it has become accustomed to. That doesn't include the cost of periodic veterinary visits, any special needs the horse might have, transportation, nomination fees for races, and insurance. (It cost $2.2 million a year to insure Affirmed after he had been syndicated.)

Thoroughbred horses are professional athletes. No capital asset depreciates as fast or is as capable of self-destruction as a Thoroughbred horse. A filly purchased for breeding may be as barren as an empty barrel. A champion runner may be lame in its stall on the morning of a race. Swale, the winner of the Kentucky Derby in 1984, finished a workout in preparation for the Belmont and fell dead. Even in optimum circumstances, the timeline on the initial investment in a racehorse is incredibly long:

1985—Mare bred to stallion.

1986—Mare gives birth.

1987—Foal sold as yearling.

1988—Owner decides not to race him as two-year-old.

1989—First year of racing, as a three-year-old. Five years, five long years must pass before the owner can find out whether his horse is a winner or not, whether his investment is good or not. It is also the case in breeding that a champion's first progeny are often much less successful than later offspring, so the timeline on the original investment may extend even longer.

Feeding, raising, teasing, breeding, training—it's all the same, whether the owner has a thousand acres of pasture and a new $6 million barn with oak-paneled interiors and brass railing, or a grass patch and an old wooden tobacco shed with cobwebs. What makes it go is the never-ending hope to have a champion horse, one that might win the Derby. Out of more than 42,000 yearlings in the country, only one will win the Kentucky Derby and have a chance at the Triple Crown of racing. But never mind the odds, or in spite of them, it is part of the genetic make-up of the Thoroughbred owner—whether he is watching a newborn foal or a three-year-old being trained to break from the starting gate for the first time—to feel a sudden rush of excitement and to wonder, "My God, could I have a Kentucky Derby winner?"

". . . if you can imagine a track that's like a bracelet of molten gold encircling a greensward that's like a patch of emerald velvet . . . all the pretty girls in the state turning the grandstand into a brocaded terrace of beauty and color such as the hanging gardens of Babylon never equalled . . . all the assembled sports of the nation going crazy at once down in the paddock . . . the entire population of Louisville and environs with one voice begging some entry to come on and win . . . and just yonder in the yellow dust the gallant kings and noble queens of the kingdom, the princesses royal, and their heirs apparent to the throne, fighting it out . . . each a symphony of satin coat and slim legs and panting nostrils . . . each a vision of courage and heart and speed . . . each topped as though with some bobbing gay blossoms by a

You Ain't Never Seen Nothing

silken-clad jockey . . . but what's the use? Until you go to Kentucky and with your own eyes behold the Derby, you ain't never been nowheres and you ain't never seen nothin'."—Irvin S. Cobb, Kentucky newspaper man, from *The Kentucky Derby Diamond Jubilee, 1875–1949,* by Brownie Leach, Gibbs-Inman Co., Louisville, 1949.

We return briefly to the scene in colonial Kentucky of two farmers standing on each side of a fence admiring his own horse grazing nearby and each thinking his horse to be better than the other. They drink a few sips of Kentucky whiskey, and before long, they are challenging each other as to which horse is faster, or which horse has more stamina. Pride in one's own horse gallops far ahead of the fall! In no time, the rivalry extends outward, one town matching its champion horse against another town's; one state against another's, the South against the North, America against England. In its simplest form, such races required only relatively open space, two riders, and not much time away from regular work. What evolved was a sport vastly more complicated and colorful in its trappings, but essentially unchanged from its primitive form.

From archaeological findings, it is clear—the mystique of Kentucky-bred racers notwithstanding—we cannot claim that Kentuckians invented horse racing. Ancient tablets have been found that indicate Assyrian kings in Asia Minor kept full stables and employed professional trainers 3,300 years before the first Kentucky Derby was run in 1875. (There is some question as to whether the earliest racing was chariot or horseback. Some argue that for thousands of years the horse was too small to carry the weight of man on his back. Others counter that it would have been unnatural for man—who, himself, has been of varying sizes through the ages—not to have instinctively mounted a horse (especially nomadic tribesmen) and, using a braided vine or rawhide thong, ridden and raced him before turning to more complex arrangements involving chariot harnesses.)

There is evidence man was riding horseback in Egypt about 1345 B.C. Achilles is known to have raced against horses in 1194 B.C., the final year of the Trojan War. The playwright Alcibiades owned horses, and three of them once finished first, second, and third in the same race. Still, it is not precisely known when bareback riding on mounted horses was introduced. In any event, horses imported from Asia

Minor and North Africa were included among the Olympic Games after
the 7th century B.C. Modern racing, so marked by the participation
of the general public in the sport, traces its legacy to the glory days
of Rome and Greece. Mounted races, chariot races, and ''Roman
races,'' in which riders raced with one foot on each of two horses,
attracted crowds as large as 300,000 to arenas like the Circus
Maximus in Rome. Public registries included bloodlines of horses
as well as racing records. Exceptional horses were buried with honor
beneath a stele citing their records. One heroic steed achieved 1,300
victories, eighty-eight seconds, and thirty-seven third-place finishes.

There was considerable opportunity to race: Race meetings under the Emperor Augustus (27 B.C.–A.D. 14) featured 12 races a day; under the Flavians (A.D. 69–96), a gluttony of 100 races a day, from dawn to dusk, at all different distances, many of them abridged to accommodate the volume. There were professional racing officials, racing colors to distinguish stables, starting chutes, legal disputes, instances of doping, heavy gambling, and possibly even the phenomenon of off-track betting—if the practice of releasing carrier pigeons after certain races to carry the results to outlying towns is any indication. There were also riots among the spectators.

The refinements that led to its evolution as the sport of kings originated in England. Over the centuries following the Roman invasion of Britain, in 55 B.C., the English had been importing fast horses from Europe, the Near East, and North Africa. There is a record of an Englishman purchasing an Arabian filly racehorse for the equivalent of 67,000 pounds in the year 1290. As the horses were bred for war and became larger and more massive, more suitable for carrying a man in heavy armor and a coat of armor itself, they became less suitable for sport. This led to the development of a distinct type of horse—lighter and faster—better for racing.

As early as 1174, there was racing at Smithfield every Friday. Sales of horses were held where the animals were ridden by professional riders to display their speed to buyers. King Richard Lion-Heart returned from the Crusades with a great admiration for the Arabian horse. During his reign, 1189–99, the first-known racing purse was offered, forty pounds in ready gold for a three-mile course with knights as riders. In the 16th century, Henry VIII imported coursers from Italy and Spain and established royal studs in several locations. The English Thoroughbred really began to develop during the 17th century. Barbs and Arabians were imported into Great Britain and bred with native stock.

As noted earlier, the Stuarts were enthusiastic sponsors of racing. Charles II (1660–85) became known as the father of the British turf for his active participation as a rider and sponsor of King's Plates as racing prizes. It was under his patronage that Newmarket was converted from a royal hunting lodge to a center for racing and breeding. The King's Plates races were popular from the outset and accelerated the changing nature of racing. The original King's Plates were standardized races for six-year-old horses carrying what is, by

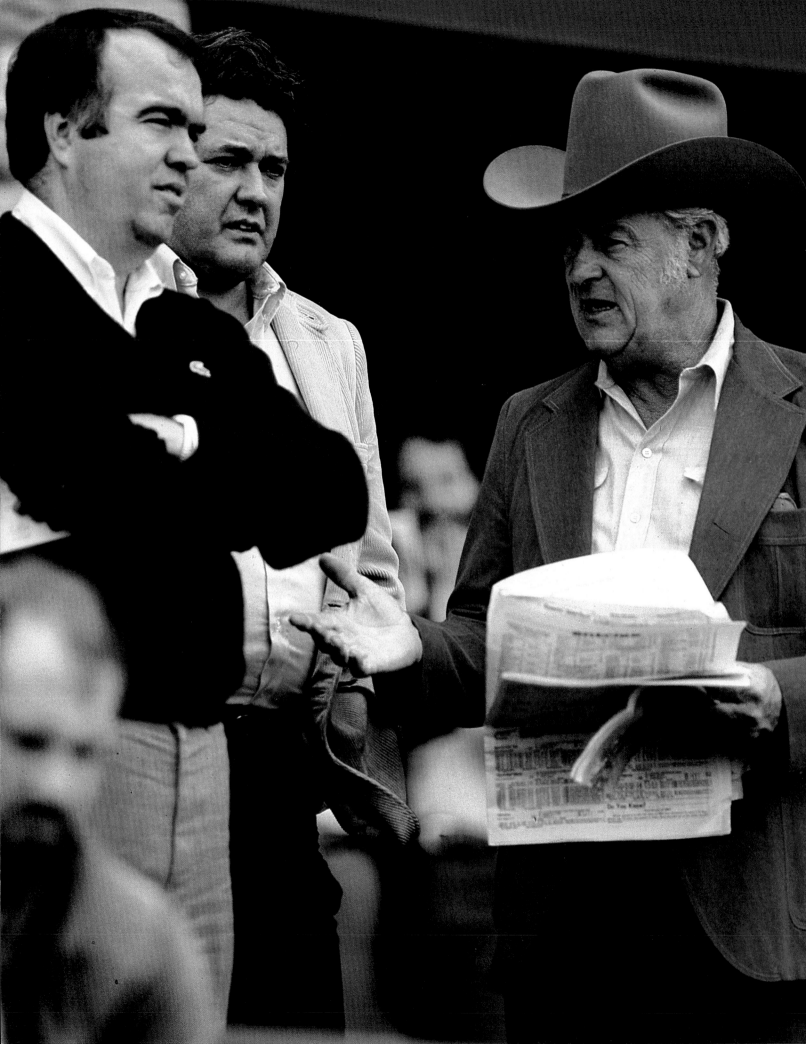

comparison with today's racing, the bone-bending weight of 168 pounds in a series of four-mile heats. The horse had to win two heats to win the match. Although it was not popular to race younger horses at first, the desire to do so gradually began to assert itself. A race for three-year-olds carrying 112 pounds in one three-mile heat was run in 1731. The younger horses were permitted to carry lighter weights.

Match races of two or three horses pitted against one another gradually lost favor to open races with larger fields of runners who met certain qualifications based on age, sex, birthplace, certain requirements for riders, previous usage, and previous accomplishments, or lack thereof. The conditions might specify "owners to ride . . .," or limit the entries to horses bred in a certain county, or to horses that had "never won plate or match of 50 pounds." These early versions of handicap races had the effect of further increasing the popularity of the sport by increasing the opportunity for more horses to participate.

King George II's Act of 1740 introduced another level of organization and standardization to racing. The legislation mandated

that horses had to be the bona fide property of the person who entered them, required certificates as to ownership and age, listed penalties for rough riding, and required riders not to dismount before arriving at the place of weighing-in. Local jockey clubs and racing commissions formed and established their own regulations. Stewards of the clubs became virtual dictators in setting policy for races. Today, the Jockey Club in England continues to exercise almost complete control of racing and breeding. In North America, The Jockey Club, headquartered in New York, though less influential than it once was in matters of policy, still has considerable influence as keeper of *The American Stud Book,* which registers foals from the U.S., Canada, Puerto Rico, and parts of Mexico. It also publishes rules of racing used as a model by many states.

Impromptu, informal racing existed in the colonies from the time of their founding. There are early reports of horse races down the main streets of towns, which provided the easiest, straightest surfaces for the quarter-mile dashes that were popular in the early years. (The quarter-mile race led to the successful breeding of the American quarterhorse, with its more compact body and unmatched sprinting speed. The animal became quite popular in the West, where it proved an invaluable ranch horse.) By the time of Kentucky's statehood in 1792, it was not uncommon for horses to race down what is now Race Street in Lexington. There were many variations of races. In some, the purse was hung from a tree and the winner was the first to reach the prize and cut it down. Creativity knew no bounds. Races were held in which each man who entered had to ride his opponent's horse. The winner was the last horse to cross the finish line. The owner riding another man's horse had to spur his mount ahead if his own horse were to have any chance of winning. Prizes were often given in kind—several hundred pounds of tobacco, a fair prize, or the loser's horse, or saddles and tack.

An emissary of Charles II, Richard Nicolls, the first governor of the New York Colony, instituted the first organized racing in this country. In 1665, he offered a silver cup to be run for each spring and fall over a course laid out on Hempstead Plain, Long Island. This was the earliest-known race trophy in North America and the beginning of course racing. The competing horses were of Dutch stock—English Thoroughbreds had not yet been imported. They carried 140 pounds and the races were run over two-mile distances. Other courses were

quickly constructed and racing soon became the popular sport of the period in New York. In New England, the Puritans were averse to horse racing and similarly indulgent activities. They especially disliked horse racing because of its association with the Stuarts, whom they saw as the incarnation of everything wrong with English monarchy and religion. Severe penalties were imposed on practitioners of "horse coursing." Connecticut banned racing. In Massachusetts and Rhode Island, social pressure discouraged its taking place. As a result, horse racing was much delayed in its development in New England, while elsewhere it grew as a popular attraction. As a variation of the above, in Virginia, horse racing was considered the province exclusively of the upper classes. A Virginia justice of the peace once fined a tailor and a physician for racing.

Horse racing as a popular, festive occasion really began in the South. Because so many of the original settlers of the South were descendants of the landed gentry of England, they were already by nature inclined toward field sports. Racing had become prominent in England by the time of the settling of America, so it was not surprising that interest in the sport migrated across the oceans as well. Their plantation-based agrarian lifestyle gave them both ample leisure time and resources to use in developing their interest in horses.

More formal, organized racing began to develop in the early years of the 1700s, and by 1750, all the principal towns of the South featured the sport. An advertisement in the *Virginia Gazette* of January 11, 1739, illustrates a race at this time:

This is to give notice that there will be run for at Mr. Joseph Seawall's in Gloucester County, on the first Tuesday in April next, a purse of thirty pistoles, by any horse, mare or gelding; all sized horses to carry 140 pounds and Galloways to be allowed weight for inches, to pay one Pistole entrance, if a subscriber, and two if not, and the entrance money to go to the second horse, etc. And on the day following, on the same course, there will be a Saddle, Bridle and Housing, of five pounds value, to be run for by any horse, mare or gelding that never won a prize of that value, four miles, before. Each horse to pay five shillings entrance and that to go to the horse that comes in second. And on the day following there is to be run for, by horses not exceeding thirteen hands, a hunting saddle, bridle and whip. Each horse to pay two shillings and sixpence at entrance, to be given to the horse that comes in second. Happy is he that can get the highest rider. (From *The American Turf: An Historical Account of Racing in the United States,* p. 18, by Lyman Horace Weeks. The Historical Company, New York, 1898.)

The first Thoroughbred imported into the American colonies appears to have been a stallion called Bully Rock, who was brought into Virginia in 1730. He had been foaled by Darley Arabian in 1718 out of a mare by the Byerly Turk. Colonial Virginians developed a reputation for fast horses. Washington Irving, in his *Life of Washington,* tells how the celebrated Colonel Tarleton got the advantage of Continental Army troops by mounting his cavalrymen on racehorses that he found on Virginia plantations.

Kentucky began to hold race meets as early as 1788. Lexington possesses the oldest racetrack in the West, having conducted racing since 1823 and having operated almost continuously without interruption, even during the Civil War, except in 1862, when Confederate General Kirby Smith occupied Lexington and encamped on the race grounds, forcing cancellation of the spring meeting. Many of the outstanding imported English racers found their way to Kentucky studs. The horses bred there thus represented the best results that could be obtained from the best stock in conditions that were considered ideal for rearing and developing blooded animals.

Prominent leaders such as George Washington, Thomas Jefferson, and Henry Clay were among the early patrons of the sport. They helped give racing a preeminence by the end of the 18th century, even in New England, where the attraction of the sport had finally overcome the strictures of Puritanism. Washington recorded his bets in his memorandum books. He acted as a judge at a racecourse in 1790. It speaks to the high esteem in which he was held that the race included one of his own horses. The same race featured a horse entered by Jefferson called simply a roan colt. It won, beating Washington's horse and several others.

The impact of a race meeting on the citizenry of a town at the close of the 18th century is captured in the notes of one observer commenting on Charleston Race Week in 1786. His observations are reminiscent of Kentucky Derby Week today.

Whether we consider the elevated character of the gentlemen of the turf, the attraction the races possessed at that time, and for many subsequent years, for all sorts and conditions of men—youth,

anticipating its delights for weeks beforehand, the sternness of age relaxing by their approach, lovers becoming more ardent, and young damsels setting their caps with greater taste and dexterity —the quality of the company in attendance; the splendid equipages; the liveried outriders that were to be seen daily on the course; the gentlemen attending the races in fashionably London-made clothes, buckskin breeches and top-boots; the universal interest pervading all classes, *from the judge upon the bench to the little school boy with his satchel on his back; the kind greetings of the town and country; the happy meetings of old friends whose residences were at a distance, affording occasions of happy intercourse and festivity; the marked absence of all care, except the care of the horses; the total disregard of the value of time, except by the competitors of the races, who did their best to save it and economize it—everything combined to render race week in Charleston emphatically the carnival of the state, when it was unpopular, if not impossible to be out of spirits, and to not mingle with the gay throng.*

Between 1825 and 1850 were run all of the great races and matches for long distances that distinguished that era of the American turf. Most of the races were in grueling three- and four-mile heats. One of the earliest and greatest racing events in the annals of the American turf was the contest between American Eclipse and Sir Henry in 1823. Eclipse represented the South and Sir Henry, the North. The South fixed itself with "invincible determination" to the task of humbling the northern champion. The race became the subject of great interest and endless discussion throughout the country during the winter preceding the event. It fueled yet again deep emotions of sectional pride and prejudice. The heats were to be held at Union Course in New York. On the day of the event, May 27, it seemed as though the entire city of New York had journeyed to the course. The South had brought five selected horses from which they finally chose Eclipse to carry their hopes and fortunes. Eclipse, who was nine years old, carried 126 pounds, while Sir Henry bore 108.

In the first heat, the Southern horse triumphed by half a length. Sir Henry rallied and won the second heat, setting up the third as the crucial race. In the final heat, Sir Henry took the lead, maintaining it throughout, and beat Eclipse so thoroughly that in the last half mile he was unable even to close for a good finish. The time of the first heat was 7:37½; the second heat was won in 7:49, the third in 8:24, for an aggregate of 23 minutes 50½ seconds, an average of about one mile in 1 minute 59 seconds. About $200,000 is estimated to have changed pockets that day, an enormous sum for that time. The entire country awaited the results. Special couriers and mail packets were dispatched from New York as soon as the race was ended. For years afterward discussion of the relative merits of the two

horses was carried on in all parts of the country with a vehemence
and persistence characteristic of the great political controversy that
was to culminate in the tragic events of the Civil War. Not surprisingly,
such sectional match races had their heyday during the period 1825
through the Civil War.

State rivalries had also become quite popular. Kentucky and
Tennessee held races that were fiercely contended. The most famous
of these occurred in Louisville in the autumn of 1839 between Wagner
and Grey Eagle. Wagner was a Tennessean, a five-year-old, while

Grey Eagle was a Kentucky four-year-old. The race took place on September 30 in front of the assembly of the most ''brilliant ladies and gentlemen ever seen upon such an occasion in Louisville.'' They had come not only from Louisville and Lexington and Tennessee, but from distant parts of the North and South. John Jay Crittenden and Henry Clay, two United States Senators from Kentucky, were there. Clay himself bred horses and had imported a stallion named Yorkshire, whose progeny had made his home at Ashland, outside Lexington, famous for the quality of its horses. A chronicler of the event writes:

The number of ladies in attendance was estimated at eight hundred, while nearly two thousand horsemen were assembled on the field. The stands, the fences, the trees, the tops of carriages and every eminence overlooking the course were crowded; probably not less than ten thousand persons composed the assembly, comprising not only several distinguished Senators, and nearly the entire Kentucky delegation in Congress, with their families, but all the elite of the beauty and fashion of the State.

By the most extraordinary exertions Wagner got up neck and neck with the gallant grey as they swung round the turn into the quarter

stretch (of the second heat, Wagner having won the first). The feelings of the assembled thousands were wrought up to a pitch absolutely painful. Silence the most profound reigned over that vast assembly as these noble animals sped on as if life and death called forth their utmost energies. Both jockeys had their whip hands at work, and at every stroke each spur, with a desperate stab, was buried to the rowel head. Grey Eagle for the first hundred yards was clearly gaining, but in another instant Wagner was even with him. Both were out and doing their best. It was anybody's race yet; now Wagner, now Grey Eagle has the advantage. 'It will be a dead heat!' 'See Grey Eagle's got him!' 'No, Wagner's ahead!' A moment ensues—the people shout—hearts throb—ladies faint—a thrill of emotion—and the race is over. Wagner wins by a neck in 7 minutes, 44 seconds, the best race ever run south of the Potomac. . . .

Thoroughbreds had begun to fetch good prices for their value as racers and in the stud by the 19th century. R.A. Woodford had created a sensation in the horse world in 1856 when he purchased for $15,000 the stallion Lexington, undefeated in all but one race but retired at 5 because of the onset of blindness. Lexington was champion sire fifteen times. His name would appear in the pedigree of fourteen of the first twenty winners of the Kentucky Derby. His name singlehandedly might have been sufficient to promulgate the reputation for excellence of Kentucky-bred horses far and wide. Fifteen thousand dollars was not the highest price paid for an import. Priam had cost $25,000. Rodolph, who never amounted to much, brought $18,000. Bertrand and Medoc were each valued at $35,000; Shark and Medley sold for $10,000, despite one wag's assessment that Shark was originally worth as a stallion about twenty shillings, and Medley, not the "cost of powder and shot that should kill him."

By 1850 or so, the growing tension between the North and the South resulted in an increased preoccupation with politics. Racing continued, but the sport lacked spirit and character during those years, "Kentucky being about the only section in which the sport flourished with anything that could be considered as approaching its normal vigor." The Panic of 1857 added further ruin to the spirit of racing, as thousands of wealthy patrons lost fortunes, hence the capacity to own racehorses. With the onset of the Civil War, racing receded into the background and appeared to linger on the edge of

oblivion. But reports of its demise were premature. Even after Fort Sumter had been fired upon, as late as June 1861, the Magnolia Jockey Club of Mobile, Alabama, announced its winter meeting for the following December and its spring stakes for March 1862.

While the war temporarily ended most racing, within ten years after its conclusion, racing had resumed. During the remaining years of the century, jockey clubs and horse associations sprang up everywhere. The period of the 1870s extending through the '80s was remarkable for the explosive growth of racing, and during this time it seemed almost impossible to satisfy the public with enough racing. There were few important cities that did not have one or more new courses opened, while the historic racing centers whose history extended back before the war seemed to renew their youth. Other important changes had begun to occur. Whereas racing had once been the domain of wealthy sportsmen, the increasing number and value of stakes and purses and the large sums of money that sportsmen were willing to pay for Thoroughbreds of distinction began to draw people who saw racing purely as a business. The immediate result of this trend was to make breeding even more important in terms of its ability to generate profits for a stable.

Another major change had to do with the races themselves. The heat races gave way to dash races, featuring younger, spirited, speedy horses who could sprint as fast as the wind. (Heat racing was a casualty of the Industrial Revolution as much as anything. In an agrarian society, a horse could be raised until it reached the racing age of four or five at no great additional expense. If the horse turned out to be a failure on the racecourse, it could be diverted to some other useful function on the farm. In an industrial economy, with its reliance on the machine, there was no easy place for a horse. The animal became an item of expense from the day it was born until it retired from racing.) Heat racing actually persisted as a popular form of racing in America much longer than in England, where it had enjoyed an earlier rise in popularity. Dash racing had not become popular in America until after the Civil War. Some of the early dashes seem to have been misnamed: They lasted for distances of eight miles, although the horses generally cantered until within a few furlongs of the finish.

Dash racing made demands upon younger horses that required changes in training techniques and in methods of breeding. It also

greatly increased interest in yearlings. The emphasis changed away from the well-seasoned, sturdy, mature racer. Sales of yearlings became prominent features of every breeding and racing season. Steadily increasing demand resulted in increased prices for yearlings. For the purposes of comparison with Keeneland, consider the prices paid at the yearling sale of the Nursery Stud in 1891. Twenty-four youngsters brought $124,550, some fetching as much as $30,000. Year by year the number of yearlings foaled grew. In 1878, the annual production of foals was estimated at 1,400, compared to the most recent modern-day total per annum of more than 40,000.

Kentucky's role as the "natural home of the American Thoroughbred" had already assumed mythical qualities by the end of the 19th century. In *The American Turf,* published in 1895, the author Lyman Horace Weeks writes (p. 166):

There has long existed among turfmen a positive and well-defined opinion that Kentucky is, par excellence, the natural home of the American thoroughbred. . . . Briefly, the contention for Kentucky is that its far-famed blue grass pastures and limestone soil offer advantages such as can be obtained nowhere else in the country, and it is particularly urged that the presence of limestone in the soil contributes to making the horses that are raised there strong in bone and capable of great endurance . . . . From the stud farms of Kentucky have come most of the great blood horses whose careers as representative American racers, both in this country and in Europe, have reflected glory upon their family and the country that gave them birth and nurtured them.

Weeks suggests that it is still "possible to raise thoroughbreds elsewhere that shall be undoubtedly of the most approved character." In any event, the establishments most renowned for breeding champions were located for the most part in central Kentucky. Among these were such historical places as Woodburn, which, as the home of Lexington until his death in 1876, was for a generation or more the largest and most successful breeding estate in the world. Most of the noteworthy horses of the 1860s and '70s came out of Woodburn. The estate of 4,000 acres had been built in pioneer days and was meant to be the ideal of an old Kentucky home. The Elmendorf Stud Farm in Lexington; Runnymede Stud up the road at Paris; Ashland in Lexington; Bosque Bonita, small, charmingly located; North Elkhorn

Farm near Lexington, which at the height of its reputation had 100
brood mares; Glen Agnes Stud—these and other Kentucky farms set
the standards for breeding and racing horses, as do the farms
of the bluegrass today.

 Just as the horses and the farms added to the Kentucky mystique,
so, too, did some of the owners, who came quickly to embody the
ideal of a Kentucky gentleman. One such figure was Colonel E.M.
Blackburn of Woodford County, Kentucky. His parents had been
among the first settlers of the bluegrass region and he had been born
in Woodford, and lived, until 1867. He devoted himself exclusively
to the raising of Thoroughbreds and was known far and wide for his
horses, especially American Eclipse and Grey Eagle. It was Eclipse
who had raced Sir Henry in 1823 for the honor of the South.
Blackburn was an intimate acquaintance of many of the famous
people of the day and enjoyed entertaining them on his farm. His
"readiness of wit in emergencies" was widely regarded. The great
statesman Henry Clay was visiting him one evening when Eclipse

was still in his stable. Clay had asked the Colonel what he could say new about the great runner. Hesitating for a moment, then rising to his feet and lifting his glass, he had replied in his most courtly manner: "Eclipse, among horses, as Henry Clay among men."

Another citizen of Woodford County—and there were many of that county whose accomplishments in racing and breeding dominated the sport—was John Harper, who died in 1873 and who laid the foundation of the great Thoroughbred nursery at Nantura Farm. Though a man of affluence, he lived a plain and unpretentious life. When he traveled with his horses, he often slept in the barn with them. He cared for them like a father for his children. His most famous horse was Longfellow, foaled in 1867 and named for the poet. Harper was not well educated and often found it harder to name his colts than to breed and train them. The name Longfellow was suggested to him by a friend, but Harper, some years later, when asked to explain the derivation of the name, had said, "We call him Longfellow because he's long and big."

Perhaps even more colorful was Price McGrath of McGrathiana Stud near Lexington, owner of the first winner of the Kentucky Derby in 1875. Another Woodford resident, he had trekked west after gold in 1849, then returned east to New York to open a gambling house. He won $105,000 in a single night, sold his business, and returned to Kentucky to start a breeding farm. Although he was a breeder of champion horses, he himself preferred to drive a team of mules hitched to a wagon.

Finally, among this very random sampling of some of the owners who helped to add to the mystique of Kentucky horses and horsemen, is the name of August Belmont. He was born in the Prussian Rhineland in 1816 to a family of great wealth and influence. He entered a banking career and came to New York in 1837 at the age of 21 to establish the bank that represented the Rothschild family in America. He became one of the leading financiers of his generation and served well in many public-service roles. A patron of the arts, he developed an interest in Thoroughbreds initially as a form of relaxing. In short time, however, he soon became intensely involved in racing and breeding. His immense wealth allowed him to buy the best horses in the world. He had originally built his stable at Babylon, Long Island, easily accessible from New York City. He enjoyed much success with his horses there, but in 1885 decided to move his farm to Lexington, where he located it on the Georgetown Pike, five miles north of town. His Kentucky operation, which he named the Nursery Stud, soon surpassed the reputation of his northern farm. (In 1917—long after Belmont's death, a colt named Man o' War was foaled at the Nursery Stud.) He bred a succession of Thoroughbreds that were among the most successful racers in the closing decade of the century. By 1889, the year before he died, twenty-three horses carried Belmont's maroon and scarlet colors. Twenty-one of them were home bred. Among them, they won fourteen stakes races that year. Belmont also helped to bring order and sense to the organization of the sport. As a nonnative of Kentucky, he was one of the forerunners of the moguls of today who live elsewhere in the world, but, by dint of their wealth, the speed of transportation, and their own often-relentless travel schedules, maintain farms in Kentucky to which they return periodically to attend to their horses.

Kentucky had the most renowned breeding farms, the most famous owners and trainers, even the bones of the most famous dead horses. Not unlike the Romans, Kentuckians have often honored their favorite champions in death. The grave of the famed Lexington is marked by a marble shaft, the first such memorial erected in this country over the remains of a champion horse. Monuments stand above the graves of the famous Ten Broeck and Longfellow. Man o' War is memorialized by a statue at the Kentucky Horse Park in Lexington. When it was announced last year that the incomparable John Henry would retire from racing and return to Kentucky, the governor of the state was on hand to welcome the gelding home.

Prominent in all facets of breeding and racing, Kentucky came naturally to have the preeminent event among horse races. In 1875, M. Lewis Clark, an enterprising grandson of William Clark, one of the leaders of the Lewis and Clark Expedition, selected the bustling river port of Louisville as the site for a horse race that he hoped would rival in prestige and significance the great races of England, like Epsom Downs, which he had visited. (The Saratoga racetrack was the only other American racecourse at the time.) He purchased 110 acres outside the city limits from a family named Churchill and called the racing association the Louisville Jockey Club. Several years later, a writer referred to the track as Churchill Downs, and the name stuck. Clark named his featured race the Kentucky Derby.

The race proved popular from the outset with owners and
spectators alike. The inaugural Derby on May 17, 1875, drew fifteen
three-year-old horses and a crowd of ten thousand spectators.
Aristides, a little red horse standing a fraction over fifteen hands and
wearing boots or protective spats, stood off a challenge by Volcano
over the 1½-mile distance to win a punch bowl worth $1,000 and
a purse of $2,850. Two hundred dollars was awarded the owner of
the second-place horse. The chestnut colt was by Leamington out
of Sarong, by the omnipotent Lexington, and was the first of fourteen
of his offspring to win the race.

The race continued to be popular and to attract horses and racing

interest up and down the eastern seaboard until an incident in 1886 threatened its future. That year, ten horses, seven of them Kentucky-bred, entered the race, which ended in a furious whipping finish between Ben Ali and Blue Wing, Ben Ali winning by half a length. Another of Lexington's progeny, the brown colt was owned and trained by James Ben Ali Haggin of Elmendorf Farm in Lexington. Haggin had been prevented from betting on his horse by a boycott of Louisville bookies. When he complained to the track officials, they were unsympathetic. He decided to retaliate by pulling his stable out of Louisville and boycotting the race thereafter. Many of his prominent eastern racing friends left with him. As a result, over the remaining years of the century, the quality of racers entering the Derby declined. One year, an eastern writer described the race as a contest of dogs. In 1899, Clark died, and by the next year, there was talk of closing down Churchill Downs.

In 1902, Colonel Matt J. Winn was persuaded to give up a successful tailoring business and take over the management of Churchill Downs. Described as faultlessly sartorial, and as having drunk deep of the draughts of life, he enjoyed immensely being Kentucky-born and -raised, especially the tradition of drinking good juleps. He was also a master promoter who had seen every Kentucky Derby. His vision and his energy soon restored fresh luster to the fading event. He built a new grandstand with romantic twin spires and gave the track a facelift. In a short time, the eastern stables returned to the Derby and the event started to grow again in its appeal.

Last year, some 109 years after the running of the first Kentucky Derby, there were 342 days of Thoroughbred racing in Kentucky, the seventh largest total of racing days among the twenty-eight states in the country that feature Thoroughbred horse racing. New York is first. There are thousands of races in this country each year, thousands more the world over. With so many races, new and old, there is still only one race that represents the perfect mix of tradition, champion horses, top jockeys, and big money. It is the Kentucky Derby. In baseball, the New York Yankees represent tradition and quality. In tennis, there is Wimbledon. In sailing, the America's Cup . . . and in Thoroughbred horse racing, the Kentucky Derby. Each symbolizes excellence, a level of competition, ability, and effort, a potential for honor and glamour unrivaled within the sport. No horse

owner, no trainer or jockey, no person who considers himself to have more than a passing curiosity in the major sports spectacles of our culture has seen anything until he's seen them run for the roses.

The history of the Kentucky Derby has been as rich and varied as the sport it epitomizes. A visitor to the newly refurbished Kentucky Derby Museum at Churchill Downs can find a wealth of information and anecdotes about the race. It is worth highlighting some of these to capture the flavor of the Derby:

– In 1889, the Derby was won by a Montana-bred colt named Spokane. Among the spectators at the race was Frank James, the older brother of Jesse James. He wore a Prince Albert suit and a soft white hat and won $2,400 on an early race. He bet on Spokane to win, putting down $5,000. The horse paid $34.80 to win on a $2 ticket.

– In 1895, the web barrier was introduced as a starting gate. The fabric wall was stretched across the track. The horses walked up behind it and the starter triggered a mechanism that caused the barrier to spring up, drawn by the force of rubber bands. In the earlier races, the horses had been required to stand even before the starter would drop the flag, crack a bullwhip, or shoot a pistol to start. A drum tap started the first Derby. Variations on starting the Derby included a web barrier stretched between motorized carts (1925) to facilitate walkup starts and to allow flying starts; boxes between horses to prevent interference; and, finally, in 1932, the invention of the modern starting gate.

– In 1896, the length of the race was shortened from 1½ miles to 1¼, its current length.

– In 1901, His Eminence became the first winner to wear the blanket of roses that is now awarded traditionally.

– In 1904, Elwood won the Derby, the first horse bred and owned by a woman.

– In 1907, a parimutuel machine was installed and saved the Derby again, this time from the local politicans and reformers who wanted to close the track and outlaw bookmaking.

– In 1911, Meridian, a New York Thoroughbred, won the Derby, marking the official return of eastern stables to Louisville.

– In 1913, a horse named Donerail went off at 91-1 and came from behind to win. He returned $184.90 on a $2 investment, the largest payoff in Derby history.

    – In 1924, an Oklahoma colt named Black Gold won. The colt was owned by Rosa and Al Hoots, who had traded eighty acres for Black Gold's mare Useeit, whom they had later entered in a claiming race. The horse had been claimed, but Hoots refused to honor the claim, arming himself with a shotgun and hiding the horse. He was subsequently suspended from racing.

    – In 1918, admission to the track was $2.20 for men, $1.65 for women. This date marked the first appearance of women in the betting shed.

    – In 1920, the track enjoyed its first million-dollar betting day.

    – In 1934, the Derby purse was reduced from $50,000 to $30,000 because of the Depression.

    – From 1938 to 1958, eight of the Derbys were won by horses trained by Ben Jones and/or his son Jimmy of Calumet Farm. Calumet's colors—devil's red with blue collar and blue hoops on the sleeves—dominated the winner's circles in most of the major races during those two decades.

    – In 1968, Dancer's Image won, but a postrace urine test revealed the presence of a prohibited drug and the horse was disqualified, giving the victory to second-place Forward Pass.

– Attendance at the Centennial of the Derby in 1975 was 163,628 people.

– Only two fillies, Regret in 1915 and Genuine Risk in 1980, have ever won the Derby.

– Jockeys Eddie Arcaro and Bill Hartack have each won the Derby five times and are the only two riders to have done so.

– Churchill Downs has forty-four barns with 1,200 stalls.

– A genuine Kentucky Derby mint julep must be served in a frosted silver julep cup. Its ingredients must all be native to Kentucky: ice from limestone spring water; bourbon at least eight years old; and mint picked after the most recent dawn, when the dew is still fresh on the leaves.

– Loading the starters into the gates at a modern Derby takes about four minutes.

– A limit of twenty horses can enter the race.

– The race is for three-year-olds.

– The owner of a Kentucky Derby horse must pay a nomination fee of $200, an entrance fee of $10,000, and a starting fee of $10,000, a total of $20,200. The money is contributed to the purse. Churchill Downs puts up $250,000 toward the purse.

– The traditional Kentucky Colonel barbecue, which occurs the Sunday after the Derby, is for Kentucky colonels only and their guests. More than 5,000 attend. The barbecue features burgoo, a stew of forty or fifty ingredients, country ham with red-eye gravy, smoked ribs, Bibb lettuce, marinated strawberries, cheese grits with a touch of garlic, and Derby pie, a concoction of whiskey-flavored chocolate chips.

– In the modern-day Derby, all male horses carry 126 pounds and all fillies carry 121.

– The Derby is also known as "one and one-quarter without any water."

– The track at Churchill Downs has a top cushion of three inches, which consists of 75 percent sand, 23 percent silt, and 2 percent clay. The next five inches is compacted sandy loam, the same material as above, atop twelve inches of clay base, which overlays twenty-five feet of native sandy loam base. The Ohio River bottom-land dirt is considered so good for horses to run on that other tracks buy it.

An ideal track gives and does not "take." In other words, if the track is too hard, it will not cushion the blows of the horses' hooves and can cause lameness. If it is too soft or loose, it absorbs the impact of the hooves but does not give back anything and can also cause lameness. The track at Churchill Downs is usually watered in clear weather after each race, not just to keep down dust but to maintain spring in the cushion. Four water trucks pour 6,000 gallons on the track after each race. The track is harrowed with a spiked drag to a depth of three inches to make the footing soft and spongy. The track is considered one of the safest in the sport. (California tracks are thought to be faster, perhaps because the climate is drier and the dirt tends to pack harder.) Horses appear to run better on grass, which is not as practical as dirt to keep up. Nonetheless, Churchill Downs began construction of a grass track last year.

The Derby itself is held on the first Saturday in May and is the eighth race on a card of ten races that day. The citizens of the

backstretch at Churchill Downs go quickly about their business
in the early hours of daybreak. Blacksmiths come and go, along
with veterinarians, horse dentists, trainers, grooms, owners,
and sportswriters looking for a scoop. Stable hands walk that day's
racers to stretch out their muscles and get rid of the kinks. They are
then groomed and fed a small portion of oats. Their main meal will
come after the race. The average horse races about twenty-five times
a year, as often as once a week when it is in top form. Out on the
track, daybreak reveals a mist full of dark forms moving up and
down the track. The exercise boys work the horses that won't be
racing that day. They gallop through the mist in perfect staccato
beats. Sounding like some unnatural distant thunder, the rumble
begins uptrack in the mist, approaches, sweeps by and away,
diminishing as the mist closes around the animal and rider—one
figure just as the Indians of Mexico saw them.

That afternoon, when the race time is near, the horse is led to the
paddock, where it will be saddled by the trainer, an age-old custom.
The owner and the trainer and the jockey will converge on the
paddock for any last-minute consultation about the strategy
for the race.

The jockey. The Lilliputian athlete. In the longer match races
popular in the early history of racing, the jockey is virtually ignored.
That is not surprising. In the longer distances, a rider's skill was
inclined to be less evident. If a horse was boxed in over a four-mile
heat, for instance, there was no hurry to extricate him. The rider did
not often have to make the kind of split-second decision that modern
short dash races require. The practice of allowing relatively large
weights on horses in the longer races indicates that small size and
lightness were not considered virtues by owners in those days.
Gradually, however, a few owners began using small boys in their
races. In 1844, a lad named Kitchener rode Red Deer in the Chester
Cup in England. He weighed fifty-six pounds and Red Deer won by
five lengths. That caught the attention of others, and for a long time it
was popular to use the tiniest of boys as jockeys. The practice in its
extreme ended when Parliament established a minimum weight of
seventy-seven pounds that a horse must carry. In this country, today,
The Jockey Club does not permit the granting of licenses to jockeys
under age sixteen.

During the 19th century in America, the South had been the center of racing. Black servant boys had done most of the training, grooming, and riding of horses. The smallest and lightest-weight of them were recruited as the first riders. America's most famous black jockey was Isaac Murphy, who showed 628 winners, including three Derby winners, in 1,412 races, for a phenomenal 44 percent. He retired early, in 1896, in part because of a weight problem. Otherwise, the annals of top jockeys in this century are missing the names of black jockeys. As racing became more fashionable and popular, blacks lost out to whites as riders, especially in gala races like the Derby. It is worth noting that from 1875 to 1903, black jockeys won fifteen of the Derbys.

It wasn't until the mid-1800s that the jockey's name began to appear in racing reports. As the shorter races came into vogue, the jockey's role in influencing the outcome became more apparent, thus more appreciated. In a dash, the jockey who wanted to win had to know how to deal with the traffic jams that could occur suddenly and terribly in the backstretch as the runners pounded for home. The great rider was the one who, when he spotted the narrow opening, abandoned any concern for safety and went for it without wasting time. Such a jockey was no substitute for good horseflesh, but he could make a difference in how the horse fared.

In the aftermath of the Civil War, as horse racing became popular once again, a cadre of professional jockeys developed in this country and soon achieved wide acclaim for its riding exploits. One in particular was James F. Sloan, known as Tod. He combined courage, skill, and judgment to become extremely successful and influential. During the season of 1896, he rode 442 mounts, winning 132 races and placing in 132 others. In 1897, riding in California, he won four races in a single day, three of them by a nose. He had once earlier, at the Parkway track in Brooklyn, ridden every winner on the program with the exception of a single jumping race. In the fall of 1897, he raced in England. He had a habit of shortening his stirrups and leaning forward to place most of his weight over the withers of the horse, thus getting his weight up onto the shoulders of the horse and off the center of its back. This style, which made him appear much like a monkey on a stick, was ridiculed by the English press. He won handily, though, and was soon emulated by riders everywhere. The style of riding has remained basically the same today. Today's jockeys use shortirons, sit lightly on the withers, and roll their hands

on the horse's neck, trying to keep their body still and to flow with the horse.

From the very beginning, the sport has been dangerous and life-threatening to the tiny men who ride the animals. And many have died, or suffered injuries that have crippled them with lifelong pain. Even the most successful—Johnny Longden, Ted Atkinson, Willie Shoemaker, Willie Hartack, Eddie Arcaro, Manuel Ycaza, Laffit Pincay, Angel Cordero, to name a few—have fallen not once or twice, but time and time again. When a horse breaks down, it's like a car suffering a tire blowout. Sometimes the jockey has a chance. If he can pull the horse's head up and try to get its weight off the broken leg, get it hobbling onto its good leg, he might be able to jump off. But, most of the time, it happens so quickly the jockey doesn't have a chance. The horse throws him—onto his shoulder, his back, his chest, his head, his neck. If it happens with horses behind him, there is the added peril of having a horse step on his head or strike him with its hooves. Most veteran jockeys have broken several bones during their careers. Falling is something the jockey tries not to think about.

The mechanized starting chute is probably the most dangerous area of the modern racetrack for the jockey. The horses are often nervous and restless in their cages. They have been known to flip over backward in the gate; to buck off the jockey and mash him into the sides of the chute; to bolt from the gate and try to jump the rail of the track.

The most successful modern jockeys, the multimillion-dollar winners, like those mentioned above, deserve their due. They dwell at the top of a monstrous pyramid whose base continues to expand as more and more horses are foaled and raised to race. The milieu below the peak, as in any sport, is the turf of an army of no-name jockeys riding nameless horses at county fair meets and small-town racetracks. Men, and now women, who are happy to win a $1,600 claiming race. If they can get mounts, they will ride 365 days a year to earn a living. If a jockey takes a vacation, takes off Christmas or Thanksgiving, and the horse he would normally ride is ridden by someone else and wins, the owner may start forgetting about him. The jockey returns, but the owner may not want to risk changing his luck. The average jockey rides a circuit, traveling from one race meeting to the next. He leaves his family for weeks at a time. For example, he journeys to Churchill Downs for the fall meeting in late October. He may go next to New Orleans to race there from Thanksgiving through April, then to Latonia in Kentucky for a month, then to Keeneland and Churchill Downs for its spring meeting, and around again. In each city, he checks into a motel, where he will live during the race meeting. He pays his own lodging and meals. For many, it is a lonely life with lots of time to kill waiting. If he is inclined to gain weight, he must maintain constant vigilance. Some jockeys live on the edge of the precipice. Laffit Pincay subsists on grains, nuts, vitamins, and a piece of fish once a week. Those who cannot stand the self-denial will eat and then regurgitate. As they grow older, toward middle age, controlling their weight becomes harder and harder. If they are injured and required to remain immobile for any length of time, they may grow out of a job. It is the matter of weight that often causes a jockey to retire even though his riding skills remain intact.

The average workaday jockey may ride anywhere from two to six horses in a single afternoon, hop in his car, and drive to another racetrack to ride several more horses that evening, as many as 1,200 horses a year. If he can win 150 to 200 of those races, he stands to make a decent buck. The standard fee for nonstakes races for most jockeys is about $35 a mount. In Kentucky, and most other places, the winning jockey gets 10 percent of the purse for winning, 5 percent for place and show for purses over $10,000. The median purse in this country two years ago was $6,100.

In 1824, English jockey Benjamin Swift received nearly $5,000, raised by subscription for his victory aboard Jerry in the St. Leger. There are scattered instances in the history of the sport of other noteworthy sums, but more often than not, a successful jockey received his wages in the form of a side of bacon, or a bag of potatoes, or a half cheese or a barrel of home-brewed ale. More charitable or richer owners bestowed presents of gold watches, diamond rings, and scarf pins set with rubies, perhaps a riding horse, a dog-cart, even a yacht, or a suit of clothes, a new hat, a box of cigars, or a case of champagne. Compare them to today's standards. In 1951, Eddie Arcaro's mounts earned more than $1.8 million in purses, to lead all others. In 1983, the leading money-winning jockey was Angel Cordero Jr., who captured more than $10 million in purses.

The best jockeys are like the best athletes of any sport. Each has

his own style: Arcaro was so smooth he resembled "split silk" on a horse; Earle Sande, who won three Derbys, seemed to flow with his mounts; Hartack in a stretch drive looks so awkward he is said to resemble a sack of wet wash in the saddle; while Ycaza "resembles nothing so much as a demon trying almost maniacally to lift his horse home." (From *Inside Racing* by Mel Heimer.) As different as each is, they are also alike. They combine superior courage and physical condition, great body strength, especially in their hands, athletic ability, and intelligence to achieve success.

These attributes notwithstanding, even the best jockeys seldom ride more than one winner for every five mounts. Ted Atkinson once had fifty-five mounts without a victory. To maximize their chances, they study the races closely. They know their horses, and they know the strategies. In fact, strategy figures significantly in a horse race. Bill Daly, a turn-of-the-century trainer, used to advise his jockeys to go to the front and try to improve their position. There's more to it than that, though. The typical Thoroughbred is capable of sprinting only a quarter mile or so at top speed. The strategy of racing lies in figuring when to make that burst. It depends on the horse, on the length of the race, on the condition of the track, and on the nature of the competition. If the jockey makes his move too soon, his mount may not be able to sustain it. Or, if he makes his move with a wall of horses in front, or on a turn, he will lose advantage. The strategy may be to set a false pace. The jockey allows another, slower horse to run in front unchallenged, to set the pace, while he tucks in behind it and bides his time. It's a strategy known as "lookin' and cookin'." The plan is to exert so little he is fresh enough to repel any challenges at the end. Eddie Arcaro was riding Devil Diver in the 1944 Manhattan Handicap at Belmont Park. It was a 1½-mile race against some of the best "stayers" in the sport. Arcaro let another horse set a nag's pace and then, with a half mile to go, sprinted the remaining distance and won handily. Some horses wait until the final stretch, then pull themselves to the front. Whirlaway was notorious for running behind, then storming ahead to win. In the 1941 Kentucky Derby, he was fourth with less than a quarter mile to go. He burst out of the pack and won by three lengths.

The other perils of being a jockey include the other jockeys. This is less the case today than was once so. The instant-replay camera that films all races has virtually eliminated dirty riding, though fouls

themselves continue unabated, more as a result of the intense desire
to win than deliberate dirty play. The stewards regularly review films
of each race, and when one jockey accuses another of fouling, they
act as judge and jury. They have the power to suspend, to take away
the jockey's livelihood. It is a power that is not lightly regarded by the
jockeys. It was a different story in the pre-film days. Olin Gentry, the
trainer, was also a professional jockey in the West and in Mexico
in the early decades of the 1900s. An octogenarian who lives in
Lexington, he remembers the rough tactics of early races. In a close
race, a jockey might grab another's saddle blanket, or slash him with
a whip, or, worse, cut his horse off by trying to run it into the rail.
Perhaps the most famous episode of jockeys duking it out was the
fighting finish in the 1933 Kentucky Derby. Jockey Herb Fisher
on Head Play grabbed the saddle pad on Broker's Tip in the
homestretch. Don Meade, aboard Broker's Tip, shoved Fisher away
and the two wrestled and slashed at each other down the
homestretch, with Broker's Tip finally winning the race. The two
jockeys resumed fighting in the jockeys' room afterward.

Today, the most common foul occurs when one jockey cuts off
another horse, or takes away his ground. Even here, there are
extremes. Eddie Arcaro was once suspended from racing for a year
for trying to put a competitor over the inner rail. In his autobiography,

I Ride to Win (Greenberg, 1951), he confesses he was no saint. His youth was spent leg-locking other jockeys, grabbing their saddlecloths, and even whipping them. He didn't escape scot-free, for he used to come back to the scales with whip welts as big as marbles across his knuckles.

As it has become increasingly difficult for a jockey to ride dirty, so, too, has it become harder for jockeys to cheat. Racing has had more than its share of shady characters and dealings. The incidents have ranged from actual conspiracy to fix races to indifferent and unexplainable tactics. The jockey who grabs hard on the reins and drops his horse back to last place has some fast talking to do to avoid suspension. Jockeys who don't keep working their mounts right up to the finish line face fines and suspension.

"You gotta win. If you don't win, you don't make no money," is the way that one jockey sums up the life and times of being a jockey. Be they claiming races or stakes races, jockeys can never get enough of winning. Every jockey, every time he boards a mount, knows that all he needs is one good horse, then it will fall into place. Everyone will want him.

The fans are packed into the 45,500 seats at Churchill Downs. Another 30,000 mill around the clubhouse. The rest of the crowd of more than 100,000 who regularly attend the Kentucky Derby are on the "greensward," the infield. As it was at Keeneland, much of the hat population of Kentucky and the United States is on display. It has been an extraordinary week—Kentucky Derby Festival Week. Over sixty events: a hot-air-balloon race, a mini-marathon, a high school basketball classic, a spring horse show, a steamboat race, a parade, an air show, a levee party, and a golf tournament. There are fireworks and concerts and a coronation ball. There are luncheons and dinners and speeches. Three-quarters of a million people spend upwards of $17 million on the official Festival activities during Derby Week, another $17 million on food, lodging, and entertainment in the city. Pegasus, the winged horse, is the logo of the Derby Festival. The celebration has taken wing and become one of the major civic events in the country. It is planned by a full-time office staff with help from more than 2,000 volunteers.

The call of the bugle summons the horses from the paddock to the track. Prior to 1888, getting the horses to the track was a long and tedious business. Then, at Monmouth in New Jersey, someone hit upon the idea of signaling the next race with a bugler, and the practice immediately caught on. The jockey mounts the horse and, following a lead pony, rides under the grandstand and onto the concourse for the parade to the starting gate. If it is a muddy track, the jockey may wear three or four pairs of goggles, which he will alternately flip on and off amid the flying goop of horses' hooves.

Some of the horses move submissively, their heads down, their long flanks working mechanically to move them toward the starting gate. Others jerk their heads left and right, argue with the bit, whinny nervously. The ride to the starting gate is dramatic for horse, jockey, and fan alike. In the background, the soft melody of "My Old Kentucky Home," the song by Stephen Foster played traditionally at the start of the Derby, rises above the infield. The bettors push frantically toward the windows, trying to squeeze in before the betting windows close. They may have been watching the tote board on the track infield, which calculates the changing odds as bets are recorded, and observed a sudden shift that signals the "smart money" has bet a certain way.

The horses approach the starting gate and seem to disappear as they are loaded into the chutes. The betting windows shut, there is a temporary lull—everything seems suspended. Suddenly, thirteen horses burst forward as if flung out by an awesome force. In a split second, the string of racing horses that had been ambling along the track toward the starting gate has been transformed into a dark phalanx hurtling down the straightaway on the sweeping, mile-long "bracelet." At the first turn, they are still a mass without distinct shape, streaked with the bright colors of the jockeys' silks, and the saddlecloths. The roar of the crowd fills the sky. Out of the first turn on the oval mile track, the mass begins to separate, to string apart, to take the form of a race. There, pulling away along the inside rail, are three horses blurred together as one. To the rear is another clump of racers, their heads up, their tails straight out, galloping for all their worth. The consequence of their position, is not yet a finality, but it is a grim prospect. Thousands of races and many to be remembered: the 1941 Derby with Whirlaway catapulting from two lengths back of the leader at the mile post to win by three lengths; the 1948 Derby when Citation, working long and low, "so low he appeared to be sniffing for moles," overcame an eight-length lead by his stablemate Coaltown to win; the 1953 Derby when Native Dancer was bumped at the clubhouse turn and thrown off pace, losing the only race of his career; Count Fleet, considered the classic example of sheer speed, leading from start to finish and winning the 1943 Derby by three lengths, the closest any horse got to him in his six starts as a three-year-old; the magnificent Secretariat burning the track in the record time of 1:59.2 in the 1973 Derby, the only winner under two minutes in the Derby's history; and Spend a Buck, the $12,500 yearling who won the 1985 Derby, thus fueling the always-present hope that Everyowner might have a Derby winner in his crop of no-name pedigree yearlings.

The final stretch at Churchill Downs is called Heartbreak Alley.

As the horses thunder down the track, the crowd roars at them. The noise drowns out the pounding of the hooves, the snorting of the horses, the curses and exhortations of the jockeys. The race becomes a pantomime. The noise and the action build until it seems as though the twin-spired grandstand will split part at the seams. And, just at that moment, slightly over two minutes after it started, the drama ends. A bay stretches its head across the finish line first, and the jockey rises in his stirrups. The horse continues to gallop, its head turned to the side as the jockey pulls up on the reins. Its chest still heaves, but the urgency is gone from its stride. Gradually it slows and turns to receive the adulation of the crowd.

In the winner's circle, the champion is draped with a blanket of 500 roses handsewn on a backing of southern smyalax greenery. The jockey is handed a garland of roses with three-foot-long stems, almost as big as he is. The owner and the trainer embrace, television cameras zoom in to transmit the scene to the entire nation. Newspaper writers record the moment for posterity. This is the eighty-fourth Kentucky-bred horse to win the Derby. The winner's share of the purse will exceed $400,000 (in 1984, it was $406,800). He receives a gold trophy worth $40,000. The second-place horse will receive a purse in the neighborhood of $100,000; third place, $50,000; and fourth place, $25,000.

The crowd of 106,000 has wagered $5.7 million on the Derby race itself. Simulcast wagering at more than thirty other tracks around the country has produced another $5.8 million, and off-track betting in New York and Connecticut facilities is more than $7 million, for a total handle of $20 million. Churchill Downs will take 16 percent off the top (for a straight bet; 19 percent for an "exotic" bet like a daily double) to pay costs, profit, and purses. Four and three-quarters percent will go to the Commonwealth of Kentucky for taxes.

The Derby is over for another year, but there are still two more races on the card for the afternoon. Still time for two more horses to win; time to recoup some of those lost bets or parlay the winnings into more; time to sit in the clubhouse and drink another mint julep; time to wander the backstretch now quietly awaiting the next morning, when life at the track will renew itself yet again; time to search out the stall of Hip #215 and to pat his nose and wonder if next year he will stand in the winner's circle, another in the long line of Kentucky-bred Thoroughbred winners.

Acknowledgments

I relied heavily on the following sources, in many instances quoting directly or adapting where suitable.

Getting Ready for Company

I am indebted to the following individuals who were very helpful in connection with this chapter and with subsequent chapters: Ted Berges, General Manager at Stone Farm, in Paris, Kentucky; Sue Richardson Early, yearling manager at Pillar Stud, in Lexington; Diana Gurley, research director at the Kentucky Thoroughbred Association, in Lexington; Arthur Hancock, owner of Stone Farm; Harold Helm, realtor, auctioneer, partner RE/MAX Auction Team, Louisville, Kentucky; Kent Hollingsworth, Editor of *The Blood-Horse: A Weekly Magazine Devoted to Improving Thoroughbred Breeding and Racing;* Jim Keefer, trainer, Louisville, Kentucky; Jack Mackenzie, farm manager at Stone Farm; Dr. David Parrish, veterinarian in Lexington; Cheri Pulliam of Northwest Farm near Midway, Kentucky; Hooper Roff, partner and general manager of Indian Valley Farm in Richmond, Kentucky; and Jim Williams, director of publicity at Keeneland Association, Inc.

The Bright Pastoral Image

The title is borrowed from *Kentucky: A History* by Steven A. Channing. I have relied on Mr. Channing's book, and on the following histories, for much of the information about the early settlement of the state: *Agrarian Kentucky* by Thomas Clark; *Cities in the Commonwealth: Two Centuries of Urban Life in Kentucky* by Allen Share; and *Frontier Kentucky* by Otis Rice. The following journals were invaluable: *A Topographical Description of the Western Country of North America* (1792) by Gilbert Imlay; *Travels to the West of the Alleghany Mountains in the States of Ohio, Kentucky, and Tennessee* (1804) by Francois Andre Michaux; *The Western Country in 1793; Reports of Kentucky and Virginia* (1794); *A Description of Kentucky in North America* (1792) by Harry Toulmin; *Sketches of a Tour to the Western Country, Through the States of Ohio and Kentucky* (1810)

by Fortesque Cuming; *Recollections of the Last Ten Years in the Valley of the Mississippi* (1826) by Timothy Flint; *A Thousand-Mile Walk to the Gulf* by John Muir. My account of the Lincoln family migration to Kentucky is adapted from Sandburg's first volume on Lincoln, *The Prairie Years.*

Ancient Life in Kentucky by W.D. Funkhouser and W.S. Webb, supplemented by *Fossils* by Frank Rhodes and by reading in some general reference works, were my main sources of information about the geological history of the area. Information about the evolution of the horse and its historical role came from *Horses in America* by Francis Haines; *Man and Horse in History* by Matthew Kust; and *The Horse of America* by John Wallace.

Bernal Diaz's journal, *The Conquest of New Spain,* provided rich material about the development of the horse in America, as did Clark's *Agrarian Kentucky,* already mentioned above. I am indebted to Eaton's *History of the Southern Confederacy* for information about Kentucky during that critical period.

The stories of horse swapping are adapted quite liberally from material in *Mister You Got Yourself a Horse* by Roger Welsch.

Breeding to Win

Olin Gentry, former jockey and trainer of champion horses, was most helpful, as were M. LaDona Hudson, breeder and trainer in Bryan, Texas; Diana Gurley; Hooper Roff; and David Parrish. I relied heavily on *The Horseman's Bible* by Jack Coggins for information about conformation and foaling, and on *Horses' Health Simplified* by Peter Rossdale for pertinent medical data. *The American Turf* by Lyman Weeks is a wonderful period piece for material about the early breeding of racehorses. Steven Crist's article "Running for the Dollars," which appeared in *The New York Times Sports Magazine,* provided insight into the current problems and opportunities of big-time breeding.

Training the Four-Legged Athlete

Here again, I found interviews invaluable, especially the words and wisdom of trainer Jim Keefer. *Horses' Health Simplified, The Horseman's Bible,* and *The American Turf* once again helped immensely, as did a slim precious anthology of facts and anecdotes about horseracing called *The Turf* by Alan Ross. A *Wall Street Journal* article by David Stipp entitled "Veterinary Medicine Attains Sophistication that is Almost Human" added a valuable dimension to the material about caring for injured horses. In addition, the Museum at Churchill Downs has a well-organized and detailed display on all facets of the Thoroughbred horse.

You Ain't Never Seen Nothing

Lyman Weeks was indispensable in his detailed treatment of the early history of racing in this country. I drew upon *Sport in Greece and Rome* by H.A. Harris, and the early histories of the horse in America cited above. In addition, Kent Hollingsworth's entertaining and informative *The Kentucky Thoroughbred* was most helpful, as was his counsel in the overall project. Mel Heimer's *Inside Racing* was another primary source of assistance on the sport in its more modern evolution. *The Kentucky Derby Diamond Jubilee* by Brownie Leach and the Museum at Churchill Downs were my main sources for the section on the Kentucky Derby. Jockey Phillip Rubbicco gave invaluable information on the life and times of his profession.

Economic data on the Thoroughbred horse industry was obtained chiefly from Diana Gurley at the Kentucky Thoroughbred Owners' Association. Dan Mearns' article "Foals and Stakes Winners" from the September 28, 1985, issue of *The Blood-Horse* was the source for statistics on Kentucky's success vis-a-vis that of other states. The displays at the Kentucky Horse Park further enriched my research, as did various discussions with the Kentucky State Racing Commission.

Finally, I am indebted to John Monteleone, of Mountain Lion, Inc. Publishers, and Jon Naso, photographer, for their valuable assistance.

Dan White
Lawrenceville, New Jersey
January, 1986

Producer's Acknowledgments

Many books today are produced outside the traditional publisher-author relationship. These are books that require the skills of several professionals, each with something special to contribute. *Kentucky Bred* is such a book. *Kentucky Bred* was produced by Mountain Lion, Inc., an independent book producer that specializes in sports, health, fitness and professional topics. To bring *Kentucky Bred* to fruition, Mountain Lion relied on the many persons whose names follow. Thank you, one and all.

- *Dan White,* author and writer who researched and wrote the text that so vividly captured the uniqueness of Kentucky bred and trained thoroughbreds.
- *Bobby Frese,* editor of Taylor Publishing Company, who originated the idea for this book and let us run with it; *Dominique Gioia,* editorial assistant, who handled all the nagging details when Bobby was occupied elsewhere; *Lurelle Cheverie,* who designed the book and gave the text and photographs its stunning form.
- *Jon Naso,* photojournalist of Sports Action Photography, who took the majority of the photographs in and around the bluegrass farms of Lexington, Kentucky.
- *Debbie Van Buren* and *Maureen Swearingen* of Mountain Lion, Inc., who spent many tedious but productive hours researching, selecting, and labeling the photographs.

Also: Edgar Allen, Churchill Downs; Robert C. Alley; Ted Burges, Stone Farm; Patrick Bunyan; Alisa Dean; Bill Doolittle; Tom and Kathleen Gentry; B.J. Gooch; Becky Hranicky; Tom House; Susan Morris; Hooper Roff, Indian Valley Farm; Colonel Floyd Sager, Claiborne Farms; Cathy Schenck; Steven S. Sharp; Joan P. Snyder; Jim Williams, Keeneland Race Track; and the entire staff of Spendthrift Farms and Spendthrift Training Center.

John J. Monteleone
Mountain Lion Inc.
Rocky Hill, N.J.
January, 1986

Bibliography

A History of the Southern Confederacy by Clement Eaton. Collier Books, New York, 1954.

A Thousand-Mile Walk to the Gulf by John Muir. Houghton Mifflin Company, Boston, 1916.

A Topographical Description of the Western Country of North America (1792) by Gilbert Imlay.

Abraham Lincoln: The Prairie Years by Carl Sandburg. Dell, New York, 1936.

Agrarian Kentucky by Thomas D. Clark. The University Press of Kentucky, Lexington, 1977.

Ancient Life in Kentucky by W.D. Funkhouser and W.S. Webb. The Kentucky Geological Survey, Frankfort, 1928.

Cities in the Commonwealth: Two Centuries of Urban Life in Kentucky by Allen J. Share. The University Press of Kentucky, Lexington, 1982.

Fossils by Frank H.T. Rhodes. Golden Press, New York, 1962.

Frontier Kentucky by Otis K. Rice. The University Press of Kentucky, Lexington, 1975.

"Horse Racing," from *Encyclopedia Britannica*, pp. 1092–1100.

Horses' Health Simplified by Peter Rossdale. Arco Publishing, Inc., New York, 1979.

Horses in America by Francis Haines. Thomas Y. Crowell Company, New York, 1971.

Inside Racing by Mel Heimer. Van Nostrand, New York, 1967.

Kentucky: A History by Steven A. Channing. W.W. Norton, New York, 1977.

Kentucky Superstitions by Daniel Lindsey Thomas, Ph.D. Princeton University Press, Princeton, New Jersey, 1920.

Man and Horse in History by Matthew J. Kust. Plutarch Press, Alexandria, Virginia, 1983.

Mister You Got Yourself a Horse by Roger L. Welsch. University of Nebraska Press, Lincoln, 1981.

Rafinesque: Autobiography and Lives edited by Keir B. Sterling. Arno Press, New York, 1978.

Recollections of the Last Ten Years in the Valley of the Mississippi (1826) by Timothy Flint. Southern Illinois University Press, Carbondale and Edwardsville, 1968.

Sketches of a Tour to the Western Country, Through the States of Ohio and Kentucky (1810) by Fortesque Cuming.

Sport in Greece and Rome by H.A. Harris. Cornell University Press, Ithaca, New York, 1972.

The American Turf by Lyman Horace Weeks. The Historical Company, New York, 1898.

The Conquest of New Spain by Bernal Diaz. Penguin Books Ltd., Harmondsworth, Middlesex, England, 1963.

The Horse of America by John Wallace. Published by the author, New York, 1897.

The Horseman's Bible by Jack Coggins. Doubleday, Garden City, New York, 1966, 1984.

The Kentucky Derby Diamond Jubilee by Brownie Leach. Gibbs-Inman Co., Louisville, 1949.

The Kentucky Thoroughbred by Kent Hollingsworth. The University Press of Kentucky. Lexington, 1976.

The Turf by Alan Ross. Oxford University Press, Oxford, England, 1982.

Travels to the West of the Alleghany Mountains in the States of Ohio, Kentucky, and Tennessee (1804) by Francois Andre Michaux.

Weather Wisdom by Albert Lee. Doubleday, Garden City, New York, 1976.

Westward into Kentucky: The Narrative of Daniel Trabue, edited by Chester Raymond Young. The University Press of Kentucky, Lexington, 1981.

Magazines, Newspapers, and Other Publications

Daily Racing Form. Hightstown, New Jersey.

"Foals and Stakes Winners" by Dan Mearns. *The Blood-Horse: A Weekly Magazine Devoted to Improving Thoroughbred Breeding and Racing*. Lexington, Kentucky. September 28, 1985, p. 6679.

Keeneland Racing and Sales Media Guide 1985, Keeneland Association, Inc., Lexington, Kentucky.

Keeneland Sales Catalogue: July 22–23, 1985. Selected Yearling Sale. Keeneland Association, Inc., Lexington, Kentucky.

Principal Rules and Requirements of the American Stud Book 1985. The Jockey Club, New York.

"Running for the Dollars" by Steven Crist. *The New York Times Sports Magazine,* New York. September 29, 1985, p. 37.

The Thoroughbred Record. Lexington, Kentucky.

"Veterinary Medicine Attains Sophistication that is Almost Human" by David Stipp. *The Wall Street Journal.* Dow Jones & Company, New York. June 13, 1985, pp. 1, 20.

MARSHALL COUNTY PUBLIC LIBRARY
1003 POPLAR STREET
BENTON, KENTUCKY 42025